Fanny Umphelby

The Child's Guide to Knowledge

Being a collection of useful and familiar questions and answers on every-day

subjects adapted for young persons, and arranged in the most simple and easy

language

Fanny Umphelby

The Child's Guide to Knowledge
Being a collection of useful and familiar questions and answers on every-day subjects adapted for young persons, and arranged in the most simple and easy language

ISBN/EAN: 9783337257057

Printed in Europe, USA, Canada, Australia, Japan

Cover: Foto ©Andreas Hilbeck / pixelio.de

More available books at **www.hansebooks.com**

THE CHILD'S
GUIDE TO KNOWLEDGE:

BEING A

COLLECTION

OF

USEFUL AND FAMILIAR QUESTIONS AND ANSWERS

ON EVERY-DAY SUBJECTS,

Adapted for Young Persons,

AND ARRANGED IN THE MOST SIMPLE AND EASY

LANGUAGE.

BY A LADY.

THIRTY-EIGHTH EDITION.

LONDON:

PUBLISHED BY SIMPKIN, MARSHALL, & Co.

AND SOLD BY ALL BOOKSELLERS.

MDCCCLXV.

Price Three Shillings.

GILBERT AND RIVINGTON, PRINTERS, ST. JOHN'S SQUARE.

INTRODUCTION.

THE most common-place subjects, and those which occur most frequently in almost every conversation, are, by youth, either totally disregarded, or but imperfectly understood.

This indifference arises from the erroneous supposition, that words and subjects so constantly in use are, in a general sense, sufficiently understood by every one, and therefore that inquiries as to *how*, *where*, *when*, &c., would be redundant, and that particular information would be unimportant, or at least unnecessary.

To convince youth of the importance and necessity of a thorough acquaintance with such subjects, and to habituate them to inquiry, by tracing the connexion and bearing of one subject on another, is the object which the authoress of this volume has in its publication.

A 2

Having been for some time accustomed to the education of children, she ever found that to produce, encourage, and satisfy an inquisitive curiosity upon every subject, was attended with the double advantage—of information and amusement to her pupils.

She is aware that the extent of this undertaking is limited; but to enlarge upon the plan, and enter more into detail, would be to destroy the object of the work, which is to concentrate the more important points of information; and she would affectionately recommend to her young friends a consultation and perusal of other books, which enter more at length upon the various subjects here embraced. Many little interesting anecdotes connected with the various subjects are introduced, to impress them more strongly on the mind of the youthful learner, and render them amusing to commit to memory. For the success which has attended thirty-seven editions of this little book, the authoress is sensible that she is indebted greatly to her friends; and the sale of several thousand copies is to her a flattering testimony that it has been well received. The second edition was enlarged to double the extent of the first, and the subsequent editions have been considerably improved.

It has not been thought advisable to introduce any wood-cuts or engravings, which might take off the attention of children, for whom this little book is professedly designed; and the authoress trusts that the simplicity of the language in which the information is conveyed, renders *picture* illustration altogether unnecessary; she believes, indeed, they would not add to, but rather detract from the usefulness of the work.

The authoress cannot conclude this address without expressing the hope of meeting that reward for her labour, which of all others will be most acceptable to her,—that of having been instrumental in the improvement of the youthful mind.

ADVERTISEMENT

TO

THE THIRTY-SIXTH EDITION

THE authoress has much reason to feel grateful for the favour which her kind friends and a liberal public continue to extend to her little work: and she avails herself of this opportunity of returning them her sincere thanks. She hopes to prove her sense of their kindness by endeavouring to render her labours less unworthy of their extensive patronage, and with this view the present edition has been carefully revised.

To prevent disappointment, a good supply of this little book is always kept on hand, so that it may never be reported out of print.

THE CHILD'S

GUIDE TO KNOWLEDGE.

QUESTION. What is the World?

ANSWER. The earth we live on.

Q. Who made it?

A. The great and good God.

Q. Are there not many things in it you would like to know about?

A. Yes, very much.

Q. Pray, then, what is bread made of?

A. Flour.

Q. What is flour?

A. Wheat ground into powder by the miller.

Q. What injury is wheat liable to?

A. To three kinds of diseases, called blight, mildew, and smut.

Q. What is blight?

A. When the leaves of the plants and stalk are shrunk up and withered.

Q. What is mildew?

A. When the straw and ear are affected.

Q. What is smut?

A. When the ears, instead of being filled with grain, become black, and are full of dark brown powder.

Q. What is bran?

A. The husk or skin of wheat. Brown bread is made by leaving the bran amongst the flour.

Q. Has bread always been made of wheat only?

A. No; barley, oats, and rye, have been more used than wheat in former times; wheaten bread being then esteemed a great luxury.

Q. Do not the people in the north of England, Scotland, and Wales, live even now upon oaten cakes?

A. Yes; and from habit prefer them to bread made of wheat.

Q. What is starch?

A. Wheat steeped in water, and exposed for some days to the heat of the sun.

Q. What does this produce?

A. A floury slimy sediment at the bottom of the water.

Q. What do they do with this?

A. Clean and dry it well in an oven, or by the heat of the sun.

Q. What is its use?

A. To stiffen linen or muslin.

Q. What vegetable do they use instead of wheat, when it is scarce?

A. The potato.

Q. Is not hair-powder made from starch?

A. Yes; it is only starch ground to a fine powder and scented.

Q. What is semolina?

A. A light and wholesome food for invalids, formed from wheat flour: it also makes excellent puddings.

Q. What is macaroni?

A. Fine wheat flour, mixed with the white of eggs; it comes from Italy, Sicily, and Germany.

Q. What does its name signify?

A. A paste : it is eaten on the Continent with milk, and in soups and puddings.

Q. How do we serve it up?

A. In a dish with grated cheese, milk, and other things.

Q. What is vermicelli?

A. A mixture the same as macaroni.

Q. How are they both formed into long slender threads, like worms?

A. By being forced through a number of little holes in the end of a pipe or chest, like a colander.

Q. What makes the difference then between macaroni and vermicelli?

A. Macaroni is pressed through holes as large as a small pea: vermicelli, through holes as small as possible; and it looks like threads.

Q. Does not the same mixture appear in the shops in another form?

A. Yes; in the shape of thin broad ribbons, which are preferred by many to the piping for making macaroni.

Q. What is it then called?

A. Sassagna.

Q. Where is it brought from?

A. Italy, and it is used in soups and other things.

Q. What is rye?

A. A kind of grain which, mixed with wheat, was at one time much used for bread.

Q. What is this grain principally used for now?

A. The distillation of spirits.

Q. What are oats?

A. The seeds or grains of an annual plant well known in Europe.

Q. What do you mean by annual?

A. Yearly; or being obliged to sow the grain, or plant it afresh every year.

Q. What are the principal uses of oats?

A. To feed horses, and to make groats and oatmeal.

Q. What are groats or grits?

A. Only oats freed from their husks; they are much used to make gruel.

Q. What is oatmeal?

A. Ground oats. It is made into

cakes and biscuits and porridge in the northern parts of England and Scotland.

Q. What is barley?

A. A well-known kind of corn, the most valuable of all grain after wheat.

Q. Where does it grow wild?

A. In Sicily, and in other parts of the south of Europe.

Q. Where is Sicily?

A. A fine island in the Mediterranean Sea.

Q. What is the principal use to which barley is applied in this country?

A. For the making of malt, which is barley steeped in water for three or four days.

Q. Is this all the process?

A. No; it is taken out and lies till it begins to sprout.

Q. What is then done with it?

A. It is dried in a kiln heated with coke, charcoal, or straw.

Q. What is coke?

A. Coal burnt in close ovens into a kind of cinder, used where great heat is required without smoke.

Q. What is charcoal?

A. Wood half-burnt or charred by being heaped up into piles or stacks, covered with turf, and made to burn; but as the air cannot get to it, it smoulders.

Q. Is not charcoal useful in different manufactories?

A. Yes; when a strong fire is wanted without smoke, and for making gunpowder.

Q. What is the use of malt?

A. To make ale and beer; hot water is added to the malt; the liquor thus produced, after it has remained some time, is drawn off, and called wort.

Q. What is next done?

A. It is then boiled with some hops, which give it a bitter taste, and serve to keep it from becoming sour; afterwards it undergoes fermentation, and is put into a cask.

Q. What do you mean by fermentation?

A. It means a working, which produces a peculiar sour, over-ripe flavour.

Q. How is that flavour removed?

A. It subsides of itself; the cask is then stopped down, and the beer becomes clear and drinkable.

Q. Is it not requisite for all beer and wine to ferment?

A. Yes; and yeast is used to assist it.

Q. What is yeast?

A. The matter produced by the fermentation of malt liquor.

Q. Are there not several degrees of fermentation?

A. Yes; the first degree is vinous or spirituous; the second, acid, or sour; and the third, putrid.

Q. What are hops?

A. The dried flower-buds of a most beautiful plant, which grows twining round long poles.

Q. Where are the principal hop-grounds?

A. In Kent, and near Farnham in Surrey.

Q. What is porter?

A. A liquor made of highly-dried

brown malt and hops fermented with yeast.

Q. How long has porter been brewed?

A. Since the year 1730: a brewer of the name of Harwood invented this liquor, which was to unite the flavour of ale, beer, and an inferior kind of beer called twopenny.

Q. Was it not considered a strengthening drink?

A. Yes; and was so much drunk by porters and other working people, that it was in time called *porter*.

Q. Is not the liquor known by the name of beer a very ancient beverage?

A. Yes; for the Egyptians made a liquor called *barley-wine*, which was probably a kind of beer; and it was the favourite drink of the Anglo-Saxons.

Q. Had not the city of Chester, in the time of the Saxons, a severe law against those who brewed bad ale?

A. Yes: they were either to be placed in a ducking-chair, and plunged into a pool of muddy water, or to forfeit four shillings.

Q. Did they use hops in their beer?

A. No; hops were first used in the breweries of the Netherlands, in the beginning of the fourteenth century.

Q. When were they introduced into England?

A. Not till nearly two centuries afterwards.

Q. Which of our kings forbade brewers to put hops and sulphur into ale?

A. Henry the Eighth: but towards the end of his son's reign, the royal and national taste began to change, and privileges were then granted to hop-grounds.

Q. What is pearl-barley?

A. It is barley freed from its husks, and formed into round grains about the size of small shot, of pearly whiteness, which has given it the name of pearl-barley.

Q. What is sago?

A. The inner pith of a species of palm-tree growing in the Moluccas and Ceram.

Q. Where are these islands situated?

A. In Asia, between Australia and China.

Q. How is sago prepared for use?

A. The tree is sawn into pieces, the pith taken out, and ground to a fine powder.

Q. What is then done with it?

A. It is rubbed through a fine hair sieve, mixed with water into a thick paste, and dried in a furnace.

-Q. What is tapioca?

A. A fine flour, prepared like sago, into small grains, from the root of a South American plant called cassava.

Q. For what is it used?

A. It affords a nourishing food, and is made into jelly, puddings, &c.

Q. What is rice?

A. The seed of a grass-like plant, that grows in Asia and in some parts of America.

Q. What country produces two crops every year?

A. China; they sow it in March and July.

Q. What does this plant require?

A. A great deal of water.

Q. Is it not the principal food of the lower class of people in Asia?

A. Yes; its general name there is paddy.

Q. To whom were the Americans indebted for this grain?

A. To a Mr. Dubois, treasurer of the East India Company, who gave a small bag of this grain to a merchant of Carolina.

Q. Are we not at present chiefly supplied from America with rice?

A. Yes; and the Carolina rice is much the finest, the grains being double the size of that which comes from the East Indies, called Patna rice.

Q. What very strong spirit is obtained from rice?

A. That called arrack is partly made from it, being also mixed with toddy, which is the juice of the cocoa-nut tree.

Q. What is millet?

A. A small seed brought into this country from the East Indies, chiefly used for puddings ; it is also an excellent seed for fattening poultry.

Q. What is butter ?

A. It is made from cream by churning.

Q. What is churning ?

A. Agitating cream in a vessel called a churn, which causes the butter to separate from the milk.

Q. What is cream ?

A. The richest and lightest part of milk ; it collects on the top, and is skimmed off and churned into butter.

Q. What is clotted cream ?

A. It is made by exposing the milk to heat without boiling, after it has previously stood about twelve hours ; this produces a thick scum, more solid than ordinary cream, which is called *clotted* cream.

Q. Did the Greeks or Romans make use of butter in their cookery ?

A. No ; the ancients accustomed themselves to the use of fine oil ; and at this day butter is very little used in Italy, Spain, Portugal, and the southern parts of France, where the olive abounds.

Q. What countries are famous for their butter?

A. England, Ireland, and Holland.

Q. What is butter called in India?

A. Ghee, and is mostly prepared from the milk of buffaloes: the Arabs are extravagantly fond of it.

Q. How is butter made in Chili?

A. The cream is put into large gourds or dry skins, which are then slung across a donkey's back, and the animal is kept trotting round a yard till the butter is made.

Q. What is cheese?

A. Milk or cream curdled by being warmed and mixed with rennet.

Q. What is rennet?

A. The stomach of a suckling calf, well cleaned and filled with salt; a certain quantity of this brine is poured into the warm milk, which it curdles.

Q. How is the cheese made into the shape in which we see it?

A. The curds are pressed as dry as possible, salted, put into shapes, and again pressed down tightly to form a cheese. The moisture squeezed out is called *whey*.

Q. Which is the richest English cheese?

A. That called Stilton, which is made in Huntingdonshire, Leicestershire, Rutlandshire, and Northamptonshire. ' It owes its excellence to the rich pasture on which the cows are fed.

Q. What famous cheeses are found in almost every English household?

A. Cheshire and Gloucester, so called from the places noted for them : Cheshire cheeses are so large as often to exceed one hundred pounds' weight each.

Q. To what may their excellence be attributed?

A. To the age they are kept, the richness of the land, and the keeping so large a number of cows as to make such a cheese without adding a second meal's milk.

Q. What English cheese is thought little inferior to Parmesan?

A. That known by the name of Cheddar, made in Somersetshire, where the rich pastures afford a sort of grass which gives it that peculiar flavour.

Q. What is Parmesan?

A. The most celebrated foreign cheese, made wholly from the milk of cows feeding in the rich pasturage of Lombardy, about Parma and Pavia. It is prepared in a very peculiar way, with much care and trouble, and flavoured with saffron.

Q. What other foreign cheese is sometimes introduced?

A. That called Gruyère, made in a small town of Switzerland, in the canton of Friburg. It is a mixture of goats' and ewes' milk, and very strong in flavour.

Q. What place has rendered itself famous by presenting an enormous cheese to Queen Victoria?

A. The village of West Pennard, near Glastonbury, in Somersetshire, which, in order to evince its loyalty, resolved a cheese should be made from the milk of *all the cows* in the parish, and when ripened should be presented to Her Majesty.

Q. How was this accomplished?

A. An immense vat was constructed to receive it, with the royal arms and many other rich embellishments carved upon it. On the anniversary of the Queen's coronation, about fifty of the wives and daughters of the subscribers assembled at the house of Mr. George Nash, with *one meal's milk* from 737 cows which were kept in the parish.

Q. How much milk did this amount to?

A. Upwards of twenty hogsheads to convert into curd, which occupied the most active labours of all the contributors from six in the morning till six at night.

Q. What was the size of this noble cheese?

A. It measured nine feet round, three feet one inch across, and twenty-two inches deep. It was presented to the Queen at Buckingham Palace, Feb. 19, 1841.

Q. What is lard?

A. The fat of swine: it is melted and run into bladders that have been cleaned with great care.

Q. What is its great use?

A. It is much employed in cooking, and is valuable to the doctor in making up his ointments, &c.

Q. What is brawn?

A. It is the flesh of the boar pickled in a peculiar manner.

Q. What is suet?

A. The solid fat found chiefly about the kidneys of sheep and oxen, very useful in cooking.

Q. What are hams?

A. The thighs of pigs, salted and dried.

Q. What are Westphalia hams?

A. The thighs of the wild hog and boar, and such animals as are well fed and roam about at pleasure.

Q. Have they not a singular flavour?

A. Yes; in consequence of their being smoked some months in chimneys where wood only is burnt.

Q. Why are they called Westphalia hams?

A. Because Westphalia, a province of Prussia, is famous for them.

Q. What is bacon?

A. The sides of a hog, salted, dried, and smoked.

Q. What is tea?

A. The dried leaves of an evergreen shrub which grows in China, Japan, and Siam.

Q. Where are these places?

A. In Asia.

Q. What is the difference between green tea and black tea?

A. Some travellers tell us there is but one sort of plant, and that all the difference in tea arises from the leaves being young or fully grown, the nature of the soil, culture, and manner of drying.

Q. But do botanists agree in this opinion?

A. No; some think there are at least two species, differing in their leaves, and more particularly in their flowers; that of the Bohea, or black tea flower, having six petals, and that of the green tea shrub, having nine.

Q. What is now the prevailing opinion?

A. That black and green tea are produced from the same plant.

Q. Is it a plant of slow growth?

A. Yes: it must have reached three years' growth before any leaves are fit to be plucked; it then bears plenty of very good ones: it does not exceed a man's height in seven years.

Q. Where do the finest tea shrubs grow?

A. In Japan, on one particular mountain, which is most carefully guarded.

Q. Are not the leaves from these trees gathered with equal care?

A. Yes; each leaf is plucked separately, and when the tea is fully prepared it is kept for the Emperor's use, and called the imperial tea.

Q. Are there not three seasons for gathering the leaves?

A. Yes; the first is in March, when the leaves are very small and not a week old: this tea is very expensive, and bought only by the grandees.

Q. When is the second gathering?

A. In April: at this time some leaves

are fully grown, and others are still young, but they are all plucked, and afterwards sorted.

Q. When is the third gathering?

A. In August, when all the leaves have arrived at their full size: this tea is coarser and lower in price.

Q. Which are the principal black teas?

A. Bohea, Congou, Souchong, and Pekoe.

Q. What is Bohea, or Voo-zee?

A. The lowest quality of black tea, so called from the country in which it is produced: it is a mixture of small and large leaves.

Q. How are they prepared for use?

A. As the leaves are picked they are put into flat baskets, placed in the sun or air from morning till night; after which they are thrown by small quantities into a cast-iron pan, which is made very hot.

Q. What is then done?

A. They are twice stirred with the hand, then taken out and rubbed between the hands of men to roll them;

after this they are roasted again in larger quantities, and are sometimes put into baskets over a charcoal fire.

Q. When the tea is sufficiently dried, what is done with it?

A. It is spread on a table, and the leaves that are unrolled, yellow, broken, or too large, are picked out; the rest are packed up for sale.

Q. What is Congou, or Congou-fou?

A. A superior kind of Bohea, less dusty, with larger leaves : they are gathered with peculiar care, and are said to be beaten with flat sticks or bamboos, after they have been withered by the sun or air, and have acquired toughness enough to keep them from breaking.

Q. What does the word Congou signify?

A. It means in the Chinese, " *much care*," or " *trouble*."

Q. What is Souchong?

A. It signifies, in the Chinese, a "*small good thing;*" very little true Souchong is sold in Europe.

Q. Why?

A. Because among a whole planta-
tion, there may be only found one single
tree, the leaves of which are thought
good enough to be called Souchong,
and even of these only the best and
youngest are taken.

Q. What is Pekoe?

A. The finest of the black teas, chiefly
drunk in Russia, Sweden, and Denmark:
it is made from the tenderest leaves of
trees three years old, gathered just after
they have been in bloom, and has some of
the small white flowers of the tea mixed
with it.

Q. What sort of a flower does the
tea shrub bear?

A. It is like our wild white rose, and
its root is like that of the pear-tree.

Q. Which are the principal green
teas?

A. Singlo, Hyson, and Gunpowder.

Q. How is it generally thought that
green tea is prepared?

A. The leaves are dried by heat immediately after being gathered, then
thrown upon cast-iron plates, and very

much rubbed betwixt men's hands to roll them tightly.

Q. Is this all the process?

A. No; they are picked, cleansed from dust several times, again dried, and at last put hot into the chests in which they are packed.

Q. What does the name Singlo signify?

A. The tea is so named from the place in which it is cultivated.

Q. What is Hyson tea?

A. It has its name from the East Indian merchant who first sold this tea to the Europeans.

Q. What is Gunpowder tea?

A. The finest of the green teas: it consists of the unopened leaf-buds, which are gathered and dried with peculiar care, but at a much lower degree of heat, so that they retain more of their original flavour and colour.

Q. What does it look like?

A. Small shot, and has a beautiful bloom, which will not bear the breath.

Q. Who first introduced tea into Europe?

A. A Dutch merchant, in 1610; who obtained it from the Chinese by exchanging dried sage with them.

Q. Were they not very fond of this herb?

A. Yes; they called it the wonderful European herb, attributing to it numerous virtues.

Q. Are not large quantities of sage-leaves, dried like tea, annually exported by the Dutch to China?

A. Yes; and they esteem them so superior to tea, that for every pound of sage they allow four pounds of tea.

Q. What does its name, *sage*, signify?

A. *Wise;* the French bestowed it on account of the property ascribed to it of strengthening the memory, and thus making people wise.

Q. In which of our kings' reigns did the East India Company give the first order for tea?

A. In that of Charles II., in 1669; it consisted only of two canisters weighing 143 lbs., and was sold at fifty shillings a pound.

Q. What is the quantity now sent every year from China to this country?

A. Upwards of ninety millions of pounds' weight.

Q. Who first retailed tea publicly in London?

A. Thomas Garway in Exchange-alley, about 1660: his house was the daily resort of noblemen, physicians, and merchants, as he recommended it for the cure of all disorders.

Q. How do the Japanese use their tea?

A. They grind it to powder as we do coffee.

Q. Is not their manner of serving it curious?

A. Yes; they place before the company the tea-things, and a box full of finely-powdered tea.

Q. What follows?

A. The cups are then filled with warm water, and as much powder as will lie on the point of a knife is thrown into each cup and stirred till the liquor begins to foam.

Q. Is it then presented to the company?

A. Yes; who sip it while warm; this custom prevails in many parts of China.

Q. How often do the Chinese take tea?

A. Thrice at least in the day, and without milk or sugar. It is a constant offering to a guest, and forms a portion of every sacrifice to their idols.

Q. What is sugar?

A. The juice of a certain cane, first brought from China to the West Indies, where it now flourishes.

Q. Where are the West Indies?

A. A group of islands between North and South America.

Q. Is not sugar one of the most ancient productions of India?

A. Yes; its Sanscrit name *Sukkhar* is obviously the origin of its European name, as *Sukkhar-kund* is of sugar-candy.

Q. Which West Indian island produces the finest sugar in the world?

A. Cuba: a great number of slaves

c 2

were formerly imported every year from Africa for the cultivation of this necessary article.

Q. Is the detestable traffic in slaves still continued?

A. In the British dominions slavery is entirely abolished; in other countries it is also abolished, or much diminished; and chiefly through the great exertions of England.

Q. Did not the abolition of slavery in the British settlements cost the English a great deal of money?

A. Yes; they paid £20,000,000 to the slave-owners as a compensation for setting their slaves free; and large sums of money have since been spent in endeavouring to suppress the slave trade.

Q. What sort of a plant is the sugar-cane?

A. It is like a tall stick or reed, from eight to about twenty feet high, with a bunch of green leaves at the top, in the middle of which is a flower.

Q. How do they make sugar of this plant?

A. When the leaves begin to hang and look dead, they cut down the cane and carry it to the mill to be crushed.

Q. What is the mill?

A. It consists of three wooden rollers, covered with steel plates, which press and squeeze out the juice.

Q. Is it then fit for use?

A. No; it must be boiled several times with a little slaked lime, the white of eggs, or other things to clear it, when it becomes partially hardened or crystallized.

Q. What is next done?

A. It is allowed to cool, and then placed in casks for about three weeks, during which the coarse remains of the syrup, called *molasses*, are drained away into vessels placed beneath.

Q. What is then done with it?

A. It is barrelled and sent to England, and called raw sugar, which is the coarsest brown sugar.

Q. Is not raw sugar often refined?

A. Yes; and the refining produces

c 3

two varieties, called clayed and loaf sugar.

Q. How is clayed sugar prepared?

A. The raw sugar is converted into syrup, which is left for some hours to harden in moulds; these are covered with white sugar, over which wet clay is firmly pressed down, so that the moisture drains through the mould and takes the colour from the sugar; this process is repeated until it becomes almost white.

Q. What is then done?

A. It is dried and crushed to powder for sale.

Q. How is loaf sugar prepared?

A. The raw sugar is converted into syrup with hot water, and filtered through canvas bags, and afterwards through powdered charcoal; this makes the syrup a colourless liquid.

Q. What is the next process?

A. This liquid is boiled and placed in moulds of a conical form, in which it becomes hard and white, the coarse part draining off, and being called *treacle*.

Q. What is sugar-candy?

A. It is sugar boiled to a syrup and cleared; it is then poured over sticks or strings placed across small tubs, and baked in a very hot stove.

Q. Where do they make sugar-candy in profusion, of all the colours of the rainbow?

A. At Constantinople, where there is a street of confectioners famous for their sweetmeats. The women almost live on confectionery, and eat incredible quantities.

Q. What is barley-sugar?

A. It is sugar boiled in water, to which lemon-juice is added; and then it is rolled and twisted into sticks.

Q. Have you told me all that is done with sugar?

A. No; rum is distilled from the molasses, or coarse part of sugar, which is skimmed off when boiling, or drained from the casks in which it is placed.

Q. What place is celebrated for rum?

A. Jamaica; an island in the West Indies belonging to the English.

Q. Has not sugar been extracted from other things besides the sugar-cane?

A. Yes; during the wars of Napoleon I. sugar was made from beet-root: and juice extracted from the birch and elm has also been used when the proper sugar could not be obtained.

Q. What is coffee?

A. The berry of an evergreen shrub, which grows in the island of Ceylon, Arabia, and the East and West Indies.

Q. Where is Arabia?

A. In Asia.

Q. What sort of a berry is it?

A. When ripe it is red, and not very unlike our cherry: the berries are then gathered, and dried on mats placed in the sun.

Q. What does this cause?

A. The outer pulp, or skin, to be easily removed with the help of mills, afterwards the berries are again dried.

Q. What else must be done to it?

A. It must be roasted, ground, and boiled in water; it is then a delightful drink.

Q. In which West Indian island was coffee first planted?

A. In Jamaica.

Q. How much coffee does one tree produce?

A. Generally not more than one pound; but a tree in great vigour will produce three or four pounds.

Q. What place is universally admitted to furnish coffee of the finest quality?

A. Mocha, in Arabia: it is grown at some distance in the interior, in the sheltered valleys of the "happy" region, whence it is brought down to this port upon the backs of camels.

Q. Where is Mocha situated?

A. On the Red Sea, just through the dangerous straits of Bab-el-mandeb, or *the Gate of Tears.*

Q. How did they acquire such a melancholy title?

A. From the dismal end which there too frequently awaits the ill-fated vessel.

Q. Who first introduced coffee into England?

A. Mr. Daniel Edwards, a Turkey merchant, in 1652; he brought with him a Greek servant of the name of Pasqua, who understood the method of roasting the berries, and making them into a drink.

Q. Where was the first coffee-house opened in London?

A. In George-yard, Lombard-street, by this Pasqua.

Q. Has not Lombard-street always been a noted place?

A. Yes; it was named after a set of Lombard Jews, who settled in England in the reign of Edward the First, and whose business was to lend money *on interest*.

Q. Who now live there, and continue to do the same?

A. Bankers. Their name originates

from the Italian Jews keeping benches in the market-places for the exchange of bills, &c. ; *banco*, being the Italian for *bench*, was in time corrupted to *banker* in English.

Q. What class of people were afterwards employed as bankers in England ?

A. The goldsmiths in the time of the Commonwealth.

Q. Why ?

A. Because the rich merchants, who before the civil wars had always deposited their money at the Mint in the Tower, no longer thought it safe there, and employed the goldsmiths to take care of it for them.

Q. What is chicory ?

A. A plant chiefly cultivated in Holland and Germany : it is grown also in England.

Q. To what purpose is it chiefly applied ?

A. Its roots are dried and prepared : they are then ground and mixed with coffee.

Q. What is cocoa?

A. The seeds of the cocoa, or chocolate plant, which grows in South America and other tropical climates.

Q. Are cocoa plants and cocoa-nut trees the same?

A. No; although they both grow in the same countries.

Q. What is chocolate?

A. A kind of cake, or hard paste, which is made of the pulp of the cocoa, or chocolate seed, gently roasted and mixed with sugar, clove, cinnamon, and other spices.

Q. Where does the chocolate plant grow?

A. Chiefly in Brazil and the West Indies. The flower is very beautiful; its fruit is contained in a pod, like a cucumber in shape; each pod has twenty or thirty seeds in it, something like almonds.

Q. How are these seeds prepared for use?

A. They are gently roasted, pounded in a mortar, and ground.

Q. How is it formed into paste and cakes?

A. By the help of water, and whilst hot is put into tin moulds.

Q. Who introduced chocolate into Europe?

A. The Spaniards. The best is brought from Caraccas. It should be used new, for it will not keep more than two years.

Q. Where is Caraccas?

A. A province of the Republic of Venezuela, in South America, bounded on the north by the Caribbean Sea.

Q. What are nutmegs?

A. The kernels of a fruit which grows on a large handsome tree in many of the East Indian Islands.

Q. Where are the East Indies?

A. In Asia.

Q. What common English fruit is the nutmeg like?

A. A walnut, being enclosed in the same sort of spongy coat, which is stripped off in the woods.

Q. Does not this husk open at one end when the fruit is ripe?

D

A. Yes; and when this coat is taken off, a very fine scarlet network is seen, which is called mace.

Q. Does it keep this fine colour?

A. No; after it is exposed to the sun, and dried, it turns to a yellowish colour.

Q. What is cinnamon?

A. The dried under-bark of the branches of a species of laurel-tree.

Q. Where does this tree grow?

A. Principally in the island of Ceylon, and forms one of the chief articles of its trade; but it also grows in Malabar, and other parts of the East Indies.

Q. Where is the island of Ceylon?

A. In Asia, at the entrance of the Gulf of Bengal.

Q. At what season do they strip the cinnamon-trees of their bark?

A. From the beginning of May to the end of October; they rip up the bark with a knife, then cut it into slices, which curl up in drying, and the smaller pieces are slipped into the larger ones.

Q. Are there not persons who taste and chew it to examine its quality?

A. Yes; and it is very disagreeable work : few can do it for more than two days together, as it deprives the tongue and lips of all moisture.

Q. Is the bark of the cinnamon-tree the only part that is valuable?

A. No; the leaves, fruit, and root, all yield oil of considerable value.

Q. What did they formerly make of the oil from the fruit?

A. Candles for the sole use of the king; their smell was delightful.

Q. What are cloves?

A. The flower-buds of an East Indian tree growing in the Molucca Islands.

Q. Did not the Dutch take great pains to cultivate it?

A. Yes; and they carried on a very rich trade in this article with the rest of the world.

Q. What is pepper?

A. The dried berry of a creeping kind of shrub.

Q. Where does it grow?

A. In many parts of the East Indies : the best comes from Malabar ; the least esteemed from Java and Sumatra.

Q. How do these berries grow?

A. In clusters of from twenty to thirty, somewhat like a bunch of currants.

Q. What colour are they?

A. First green; but they change to a bright red when ripe, and after they are dried they become black.

Q. Are black and white pepper the fruit of the same shrub?

A. Yes; the berries are only dried for black pepper; but for white pepper the best and soundest of the berries are chosen, steeped in sea-water, and dried in the sun.

Q. What does this cause?

A. The skin to shrivel, which is then easily rubbed off by the hand, and leaves the berry white.

Q. What is allspice?

A. The fruit of the beautiful pimento-tree.

Q. Where does it grow?

A. In Jamaica and other parts of the West Indies.

Q. Why is it called allspice?

A. Because it is thought to possess the flavour of all other spices.

Q. What is ginger?

A. The dried root and under-ground stem of a reed-like plant. It derives its name from, and abounds in the mountainous district of Gingi, to the east of Pondicherry, and is cultivated all over the tropics of Asia and America.

Q. What plant does it resemble?

A. A rush; and the knotty root spreads itself over the surface of the ground.

Q. How do the Indians use it?

A. When fresh gathered it is soft, and in that state it is eaten by them as a salad.

Q. Does it not likewise make a fine preserve?

A. Yes; a most delicious one, and it is reckoned a great delicacy.

Q. What is mustard?

A. It is made from the powdered

seeds of a plant which grows wild in some parts of England; but it is cultivated with great success in Durham.

Q. What is the betel-nut which we hear so much of the Indians chewing?

A. It is the nut of a beautiful tree, called the areca palm, the tallest and slenderest of the species; it is cultivated all over India for the sake of the nut.

Q. How is the nut prepared?

A. It is dried and cut into slices, which are wrapped up in the leaf of the black pepper vine, and sprinkled with quick-lime; the natives chew it in such quantities, that their lips become quite red and their teeth black.

Q. Do they not consider this a beauty?

A. Yes; and they carry the prepared nut about their persons in boxes, as we do snuff, and present it to each other; this is done by women as well as men.

Q. Would they not consider it great rudeness if you refused it?

A. Yes.

Q. What are anise-seeds?

A. The seeds of an annual plant which grows wild in Egypt, Syria, and other Eastern countries.

Q. Did we not try to cultivate this plant in this country?

A. Yes; but our climate is too cold, and we obtain the anise-seeds from Malta and Spain; they are very valuable in medicine.

Q. What are cardamoms?

A. The seeds of an East Indian plant, which are brought into Europe in their pods, and are very valuable in medicine.

Q. Do not the Indians use them in great quantities in their food?

A. Yes; and they also mix them with betel, and chew them.

Q. What is caraway-seed?

A. A small well-known seed, much used by pastry-cooks in cakes, and very useful in medicine.

Q. Does not this plant grow wild in many parts of England?

A. Yes; particularly about Bury St.

Edmund's in Suffolk; and it is much grown in Essex and Kent.

Q. How do they thresh it?

A. In the fields on a cloth, in the same manner as rape-seed.

Q. What are coriander-seeds?

A. The seeds of a plant much grown in Essex and Kent, and used by distillers, druggists, and confectioners.

Q. What is turmeric?

A. The root of an East Indian plant, like ginger, used in India and Europe in medicine and in making curry powder, and seasoning many dishes.

Q. What is it chiefly valuable for now?

A. For giving a rich yellow dye to silk and linen, and improving the fine red dye of cochineal.

Q. What is arrow-root?

A. The root of a plant growing in the East and West Indies: there are three species of it; that used for food is called the starch plant, and requires a long preparation.

Q. Where is it extensively cultivated?

A. In the gardens and provision grounds of the West Indies.

Q. From what circumstance does it derive its name?

A. From the Indians using the root of another species of it, called *galanga*, as an antidote to the venom communicated by their poisoned arrows, and the stings of venomous insects.

Q. What is maize or Indian corn?

A. A grain much cultivated in America, for it yields two crops in the year, and is used for bread, puddings, cakes, &c.

Q. Is it not more productive than any other plant cultivated for the use of mankind?

A. Yes; especially in Mexico and Peru, and other very hot climates, where a single grain yields four hundred-fold.

Q. What is saffron?

A. The orange-coloured stigma, or centre part of a purple kind of crocus, which is gathered every morning as soon as the flower has been opened by the influence of the sun.

Q. What part of them is used?

A. The upper part of the stigma is picked out, and the rest of the flower thrown away; they are dried in a kiln, and made into cakes.

Q. Where did this plant abound?

A. In Essex, on the borders of Cambridgeshire, where there is a town called Saffron Walden, from the quantity of saffron which was formerly grown in the neighbourhood.

Q. Where does it now chiefly grow?

A. In Spain, France, and Germany.

Q. What is the use of saffron?

A. A yellow colour is prepared from it, used in cookery and dyeing, and sometimes in medicine; it dissolves in water.

Q. What is the orris-root?

A. A root well known from its delightful smell, which is like the violet; it is used to scent hair-powder and other articles.

Q. From whence is it brought?

A. Chiefly from Leghorn, in Italy.

Q. What is liquorice?

A. The root and juice of a plant which grows in abundance in England.

Q. In what part does it abound?

A. Whole fields of it are to be seen in the neighbourhood of Pontefract, in Yorkshire.

Q. What is Spanish liquorice?

A. The root and juice of the same plant which grows in great quantities in Spain.

Q. Where is Spain?

A. In Europe.

Q. What is wine?

A. The fermented juice of grapes and vegetables.

Q. What causes the great variety in the colour and quality of wines?

A. The different species of grapes, produced by the varieties of soil, cultivation, and climate, and the peculiar mode of fermentation.

Q. What causes the difference between red and white wine?

A. Not so much the quality of the grape, as the preparation of it.

Q. How does this occur?

A. If the juice of the red grape be carefully pressed and fermented separately from the skins, it forms a white wine.

Q. But I suppose if the skins be pressed, and remain during fermentation, the wine is red?

A. Yes; but there are white grapes as well as red, which also causes a difference in wine.

Q. What wine is much consumed in England?

A. That called red port.

Q. Where does this wine come from?

A. Oporto, a rich and handsome town in Portugal; it has its name from the city, in the neighbourhood of which the vines are cultivated.

Q. How long has this wine been so much esteemed in England?

A. Not much above a century; for in the reign of William and Mary five hundred pipes would glut the market;

now we receive annually about twenty-five thousand pipes.

Q. Is there not a wine called white port?

A. Yes; it comes from Portugal, and was some years ago much used; but now it is seldom called for.

Q. What is Lisbon wine?

A. A sweet white wine produced near Lisbon, the capital of Portugal.

Q. From whence does Madeira come?

A. From the Madeira and Canary Islands in the North Atlantic Ocean, off the coast of Africa.

Q. Is it not considered a most valuable white wine?

A. Yes; particularly after it has been ripened by a voyage or two to the East Indies: it is then called East Indian Madeira.

Q. What is Malmsey Madeira?

A. A rich luscious white wine brought from Madeira and the Canary Islands; it used to be called Canary sack, and is much spoken of in Shakspeare.

Q. Where did the vines grow which produced this fine wine?

A. In Candia, and in Malvesia, one of the Greek Islands ; they were afterwards transplanted to the Canary Islands.

Q. Is much of this wine made ?

A. No ; it is so scarce that few persons possess it.

Q. What prince was drowned in a butt of Malmsey wine ?

A. The Duke of Clarence, brother to Edward IV.

Q. Where is Candia ?

A. An island in the Mediterranean Sea.

Q. What is Sherry ?

A. A strong white wine, brought from Xeres, not far from Seville, in Andalusia in Spain.

Q. What is Mountain wine ?

A. It is a sweet, luscious Spanish white wine, made from the full ripe grapes which grow on the mountains around Malaga.

Q. What is Tent wine ?

A. A sweet red wine called Tent, or *tinto*, because it is a white wine coloured: from this process it becomes a very rich and excellent red wine.

Q. Is not Tent wine made from the juice of a particular kind of grape?

A. Yes; and the grapes are not used for the wine until some time after they have been perfectly ripe.

Q. What places produce it?

A. Alicant and Malaga: indeed, the same grapes which produce Mountain wine are used for Tent, or *tinto*, being only coloured; and this wine is known there by the name of *vino tinto*.

Q. From what place do we chiefly import this wine and Sherry?

A. From Cadiz.

Q. Where is Cadiz?

A. A fortified city in Spain, in Andalusia, with a good harbour; it is the centre of the Spanish commerce to America and the West Indies.

Q. Where is Malaga?

A. A city in Grenada, in the south of Spain: it has a stupendous cathedral, built by Philip II., while married to Mary of England.

Q. Where is Alicant?

A. A city and sea-port of Valencia, in Spain.

Q. Do not Hungary and Germany produce many excellent wines ?

A. Yes; Tokay, Hock, Rhenish, and Moselle are the most celebrated.

Q. What is Tokay ?

A. A very scarce and expensive wine, brought from a town of the same name in Hungary, near which it is chiefly made.

Q. What is the hill called, that produces the grapes of which this wine is made ?

A. The Sugar Hill; the common grapes are mixed with a portion of luscious, half-dried, shrivelled grapes, which grow on this hill.

Q. What renders it so scarce ?

A. The small quantity that is made of it, and its being principally bought by the nobility of Hungary.

Q. What German wine is in the greatest request in England ?

A. Hock: it has its name from the

town of Hockstadt, in Suabia, and is a pleasant wine in summer.

Q. What are Rhenish and Moselle?

A. They are produced chiefly on the banks of the Rhine and Moselle rivers, and have a cool sharp taste.

Q. Are not the Germans very curious in their wines?

A. Yes; before the wars at the beginning of this century, many of the nobility had wines in their cellars that were more than a hundred years old.

Q. Had they not lost all their goodness?

A. No; they had been made so rich and good, that they had remained uninjured, even by so great an age.

Q. Are not the French wines celebrated?

A. Yes; the most valuable is Champagne; it is of two kinds, still Champagne, and sparkling Champagne.

Q. What is still or quiet Champagne?

A. The wine that has gone through the whole process of fermentation.

Q. What is sparkling Champagne?

A. That which has been bottled before the fermentation was complete.

Q. What is Vin de Grave?

A. A French wine, made near Bordeaux.

Q. What is Pontac?

A. Another French wine, made in Guienne.

Q. What are Frontignac and Muscadel?

A. White wines, the delicious productions of Languedoc.

Q. From what is the name Muscadel derived?

A. Some suppose from the grape having a little the flavour of musk, and others from *musca*, the Latin word for a fly, because flies are extremely fond of its grapes.

Q. What is Burgundy?

A. A fine red wine, which has its name from the province where it is made.

Q. What is Claret?

A. A thin, highly flavoured red wine, much drunk and esteemed in England.

Q. Where does it come from ?

A. The neighbourhood of Bordeaux.

Q. What do the French call the inferior kinds of this wine ?

A. *Vin ordinaire ;* it is the common beverage of the working classes in France.

Q. What is Hermitage ?

A. A wine produced from vineyards on the east bank of the Rhone ; there are two sorts, red and white.

Q. What town in France is famous for this wine ?

A. The little town of Tain, near Lyons ; it is made from a small black grape, of a rough flavour.

Q. What is Côte Rôtie ?

A. A wine made from the vineyards on the opposite side of the river Rhone.

Q. What is Rota wine ?

A. A rich and sweet white wine, produced in Rota, near Seville.

Q. Pray, is Italy famous for wines ?

A. It was among the ancients ; but now its wines are thin and bad.

Q. Does it not produce one good sort ?

A. Yes ; that called Lachryma Christi ;

it is a luscious wine, produced from the vineyards of Mount Vesuvius.

Q. What was Falernian wine?

A. It was a wine much celebrated by the ancient poets, particularly Virgil and Horace.

Q. What part of Italy produced it?

A. Falernus, a fertile mountain and plain of Campania, a part of Italy considerably south-east of Rome.

Q. What is Constantia?

A. A very rich sweet wine, made at the Cape of Good Hope.

Q. Is there not red as well as white Constantia?

A. Yes; it is made about eight miles from Cape Town, at a farm of the same name.

Q. What causes the grapes of this farm to be so very fine?

A. Some peculiarity in the soil: the wine is made with great care, no fruit being used but what is fully ripe and in the highest perfection.

Q. When is this wine in perfection?

A. In about two years; when kept

six or seven, it ferments and loses its flavour.

Q. What is Schiraz wine?

A. A fine Persian wine, very much esteemed; the town of Schiraz is delightfully situated in a fertile plain, and contains so many beautiful gardens, that it is styled an earthly paradise, and the Athens of Persia.

Q. What people always drink their wine warm?

A. The Chinese, who also consider it a great compliment to be congratulated on their ability to drink a large quantity.

Q. What is Noyeau?

A. A delightful cordial, made of white brandy, and sweet and bitter almonds, with other kernels.

Q. Where is the finest made?

A. At Martinique, one of the West Indian Islands.

Q. What is Hippocras?

A. A costly beverage, used chiefly at royal banquets, in which the champion, out of a golden cup, pledged the king at the coronation.

Q. What was it composed of?

A. Red wine, cinnamon, ginger, and other spices, run through a woollen bag, in the same manner as our modern jellies.

Q. Why is it called Hippocras?

A. From the bag being termed "*Hippocrates' sleeve*," through which it was strained; it was so expensive that it was never presented more than once during the feast.

Q. What is capillaire?

A. A luscious syrup, formed of sugar, and a juice extracted from a plant called maiden-hair.

Q. Where is this plant found?

A. In the southern parts of France and the Mediterranean; it is an herb which grows on rocks and old ruins.

Q. What is ratafia?

A. A cordial prepared by infusing in brandy the kernels of several kinds of fruit, particularly of cherries and apricots, adding also sugar, cinnamon, cloves, and other spices.

Q. What is sherbet?

A. A kind of lemonade, made from the juice of the lime, a very favourite beverage in Egypt and Turkey.

Q. What is brandy?

A. A spirituous liquor distilled from weak French wines, which are unfit for exportation.

Q. What is the difference between wine and spirits?

A. Wine is only *fermented*, spirits are also *distilled*.

Q. What do you mean by distilling?

A. It is to draw off, drop by drop, the spirit of any body by means of fire placed above or under the vessels that contain the liquor to be distilled: the spirit or alcohol rises in vapour and passes into a tube surrounded by cold water, which condenses it into a liquid.

Q. Whence have we the finest brandy?

A. From Bordeaux, Languedoc, and the department of Charente; from the latter comes the well-known Cognac brandy.

Q. What is the colour of brandy when it comes from the still?

A. White as water; it is coloured

partly by the oaken casks in which it is kept, and partly by burnt sugar and other harmless things.

Q. Do these things affect the quality of the spirit?

A. Not in the least.

Q. Is not a large quantity of brandy made in this country?

A. Yes; it is distilled principally from malt or barley, but it is thought very inferior, though much used, as the duty on French brandy renders it more expensive.

Q. What is Hollands or Geneva?

A. It is a spirit made from grain in Holland, where the only true Geneva is distilled; it is flavoured with juniper berries.

Q. Why is it called Geneva?

A. From *genièvre*, the French word for juniper.

Q. From whence are juniper berries imported?

A. From Holland and Italy.

Q. What is English gin?

A. It is a spirit distilled from malt, flavoured with oil of turpentine, and by infusing a few juniper berries and some hops.

Q. What is whisky?

A. A very strong spirit distilled from grain, much liked and used by both the Scotch and Irish.

Q. Has it not a peculiar smoky flavour?

A. Yes; this arises from the fuel called peat, which is used to heat the still, and is a kind of turf dug off the moors.

Q. What are the various liqueurs known by the names of Eau-d'or, Maraschino, Kirschewasser, &c. made of?

A. They all consist of brandy flavoured by the essential oil of aromatic plants, and sweetened with sugar.

Q. Is not the juice of cherries used by the Germans in the manufacture of the last-named liqueurs?

A. Yes; especially in the latter, a liqueur which bears a high price in the foreign market.

Q. What is cider?

A. The fermented juice of apples.

E

Q. What counties are particularly famous for cider?

A. Herefordshire, Devonshire, and the surrounding districts.

Q. What is perry?

A. The fermented juice of pears.

Q. What counties are famous for it?

A. Worcestershire and Herefordshire.

Q. What is vinegar?

A. An acid liquor made from malt; but wine, beer, cider, &c. may be turned into vinegar, by exposing the vessel to the heat of the sun, or heating it in a stove, and thereby producing fermentation.

Q. What is mead?

A. A liquor made from honey and water, fermented with yeast.

Q. What is honey?

A. The syrup of flowers, drawn from the opened buds by the industrious bee.

Q. What is virgin-honey?

A. The honey made by the young bees, which is purer than any other.

Q. Has not the term *Honey Moon* its origin from a custom prevailing among an ancient Gothic people of Germany?

A. No doubt; for they drank mead, or *metheglin*, as it was called, for thirty days after a wedding.

Q. What is manna?

A. A sweet syrup or sap, that flows from several kinds of ash-trees, as gum does from plum-trees.

Q. How is it prepared?

A. It hardens and dries on the tree like gum, when it is carefully gathered, and used as a medicine.

Q. Where does the best come from?

A. Calabria and Sicily.

Q. Where is Calabria?

A. A district at the extreme south of the kingdom of Italy.

Q. What animals furnish man with milk?

A. The cow, the goat, and the ass.

Q. Where is goats' milk particularly valuable?

A. On board ship, where the goats thrive better than any other animal.

Q. What is asses' milk good for?

A. It is light and nourishing, and much drunk by sick persons and children.

Q. Was not the ass much valued by the Romans?

A. Yes; and though its milk was not applied to the purposes of medicine, it was early converted to the uses of vanity.

Q. How?

A. It was supposed by the ladies of Rome to contribute much, as a wash, towards whitening their skins.

Q. What empress kept a train of milch asses in constant attendance upon her?

A. Nero's consort, that her bath might be continually replenished with their milk.

Q. Whence are oranges brought?

A. From Majorca and Minorca, also from Lisbon, and most of the islands and places in the Mediterranean Sea.

Q. Are there not many different kinds?

A. Yes; but the St. Michael's are the most common and delicious; they are imported in large quantities from the Azores.

Q. Where are the Azores?

A. A group of islands in the Atlantic Ocean, about eight hundred miles west of Portugal.

Q. What distinguishes the St. Michael's from other kinds of oranges?

A. It is small, with a thin rind, and without seeds; the pulp is very sweet and juicy.

Q. How many oranges will a good tree bear?

A. From one thousand to two thousand.

Q. Where is there now an orange-tree nearly four hundred years old?

A. In the gardens of Versailles; it belonged to the Constable de Bourbon, in the reign of Francis I., contemporary with our Henry VIII.

Q. Is it very large?

A. It is thirty feet high, and branches off into two stems, each as large as a common orange-tree.

Q. What story is related concerning the first orange-tree which was the

E 3

parent of all the multitudes now in Europe?

A. That it was the only plant that lived out of a great number sent as a present from Asia to Conde Mellor.

Q. Who was he?

A. A Prime Minister to the king of Portugal.

Q. What well-known perfume is made from the rind of the orange?

A. Bergamot; it is made near the town of Bergamo, in Italy; the rind is cut into small pieces, and the oil pressed out into glass vessels.

Q. What are Seville oranges?

A. A large, bitter, dark-coloured and rough-skinned orange, much used in medicine and cookery.

Q. What common preserve is chiefly made from oranges?

A. Marmalade: the pulp of the orange is pounded, mixed with sugar, and then heated and passed through a sieve.

Q. What is the shaddock?

A. A fruit of the orange kind, as

large as the head of a child, common in both the East and West Indies: it is known in the English market as the Forbidden Fruit.

Q. From whom does it derive its name?

A. From a Captain Shaddock, who brought it from China, or, as some say, from Guinea, and planted it in the West Indies.

Q. Whence have we lemons?

A. Principally from Spain and Portugal.

Q. Of what country is the lemon-tree a native?

A. Assyria and Media, in Asia; it was afterwards planted in Greece and other southern parts of Europe.

Q. Is not lemon a delightful acid?

A. Yes, and much used in cookery, confectionery, and medicine.

Q. Are not lemons also much used by calico-printers?

A. Yes; to discharge colours from iron.

Q. What is essential salt of lemons?

A. It is a preparation made from the juice of sorrel, used for taking out ink-stains from linen.

Q. What kind of fruit is the citron?

A. A sort of lemon, only larger and the pulp firmer; it is principally used in sauces, and from the rind a delicate sweetmeat is prepared.

Q. What is lime?

A. A kind of lemon, though a much smaller fruit, about the size of an egg; the juice is much preferred to that of the lemon.

Q. Where do limes grow?

A. In North America and the West Indies, where they are to be seen at all entertainments; also in Spain, Portugal, and Egypt.

Q. Have not most of the fine vegetables and delicious fruits we now enjoy in England been introduced into it from other countries?

A. Yes; it was not until the latter end of the reign of Henry VIII., about 1546, that salads, carrots, turnips, and other eatable roots, were produced in England.

Q. What countries furnished England with vegetables before she cultivated them?

A. Holland and Flanders; the court was tolerably supplied, but the rest of the country scarcely knew the taste of them.

Q. Is not the potato one of the most useful roots we possess?

A. Yes; it forms the principal food of many of the poor in this country, and in Ireland they chiefly live upon it.

Q. To what country are we indebted for such a valuable plant?

A. It has been said that Sir Francis Drake first brought it from Santa Fé, in New Mexico, North America.

Q. But what great man is said to have first planted it in Ireland?

A. Sir Walter Raleigh, at Youghal, in the county of Cork, in 1610, in the reign of James I.

Q. What county in England is thought to excel in this vegetable?

A. Lancashire; Formby, a few miles north of Liverpool, is remarkable for producing the best in the country.

Q. What old story is related with regard to this?

A. It is said that a vessel laden with

potatoes from Ireland to London, was driven on shore at Formby, which occasioned them to be first planted at that place.

Q. Was not their progress very slow?

A. Yes; they were for a long time only grown as delicacies in the gardens of men of fortune, and even in Charles I.'s time, they are named as articles provided for the queen's table, at the price of two shillings per lb.

Q. When were asparagus, artichokes, cauliflowers, beans, peas, and cabbages introduced?

A. About the time of Charles II.

Q. Who first planted cabbages in England?

A. Sir Anthony Ashley: the plants were brought from Holland; he is represented in his monument with a cabbage at his feet.

Q. What is sour-crout?

A. It is prepared from all kinds of cabbage, and is a favourite food among the Germans and people of other northern countries on the Continent.

Q. Were not the Greeks and Romans well acquainted with these plants?

A. Yes; and they were much used and cultivated by them.

Q. Are not turnips a most useful vegetable?

A. Yes; they were brought into this country from Hanover and Germany.

Q. In what county are they now much cultivated?

A. In Norfolk; but in all parts of England they are grown, as they afford such fine food for sheep and cattle.

Q. What is beet?

A. A red vegetable of the turnip tribe, often called mangel wurzel; it affords food for cattle during the inclemency of winter.

Q. What are truffles?

A. A fungus without root, which grows at the depth of four or five inches in the earth, from the size of a pea to that of a potato.

Q. How are they discovered?

A. By means of dogs, which are taught to hunt for them by scent, and when they smell one, they bark and scratch it up; in Italy they are hunted for by pigs.

Q. How are they served at table?

A. Either roasted in a fresh state, like potatoes, or cut into slices and dried, to flavour sauces and soups.

Q. It does not appear then that our island possessed many native fruits?

A. No; nuts, acorns, crabs, medlars, cranberries, and blackberries, were perhaps the only fruits of this present garden island.

Q. Is there not a difference of opinion on this subject?

A. Yes; some consider raspberries, strawberries, gooseberries, and currants, to be indigenous or native; but if so, they were of an inferior kind to those we now see in our gardens, which were probably introduced from warmer climates.

Q. From what place had we the apple?

A. From Persia; it is produced in an artificial manner, by a process termed grafting.

Q. What is grafting?

A. It is inserting young shoots of such trees as bear valuable fruit into the stock of another tree of a similar nature, which is plastered and bound up till it grows to it.

Q. Will it then produce fruit of the same quality as the tree from which it was taken?

A. Yes; and this process is used for propagating nearly every kind of fruit-tree.

Q. What do you mean by propagating?

A. Increasing.

Q. Why do they not raise them from seed?

A. Because they would only be like wild fruit, and never come to perfection.

Q. Is the pear much cultivated?

A. Yes; it is a well-known garden fruit; the wood is light and smooth, of a yellow colour.

Q. What is it useful for?

A. Picture-frames that are to be stained black; carpenters' and joiners' tools: also the common kind of flat rulers, and furniture.

Q. What country produced the pine-apple?

A. This best and finest flavoured of all known fruits was brought to England in 1690, from South America.

Q. Where do they grow in great perfection in the open ground?

A. In South America and the West Indies, whence they have of late years been imported into England in great abundance.

Q. Where are pine-apples as plentiful as blackberries in England?

A. At Sierra Leone, in Africa.

Q. How do we raise this fine fruit in Europe?

A. In hot-houses: they are a luxury for the rich; the pots which contain them are sunk in beds of bark, after it has been used by the tanners.

Q. When is this fruit in perfection?

A. From the middle of August to the end of September; when brought to table, their leafy crown should be saved for planting.

Q. When were green-houses introduced into England?

A. In the reign of William III.; they are mentioned as a very curious contrivance to raise and preserve tender plants.

Q. Does not England excel in producing finer grapes for the table than any other country?

A. Yes; since artificial heat was applied, which was about the beginning of the last century.

Q. Did not the vinery of the Duke of Portland, at Welbeck, near Worksop, produce a wonderful bunch of Syrian grapes?

A. Yes; about the middle of the last century; it weighed $19\frac{1}{2}$ lbs., and was sent by the Duke as a present to the Marquis of Rockingham, at Wentworth House, a distance of twenty miles; four labourers carried it on a staff by turns.

Q. Is there not still a very famous vine at Hampton Court?

A. Yes, the Red Hamburgh; it has

F 2

been known to produce 2200 bunches averaging one lb. each.

Q. Does not the vine attain a very great age?

A. Yes; it is said to equal that of the oak; a vineyard one hundred years old is reckoned young.

Q. Where are the vineyards the most beautiful?

A. Between Rome and Naples; they are trained to elms and poplars from branch to branch in all directions, in the most luxuriant manner.

Q. Why are not the vineyards in France and on the Rhine as beautiful?

A. Because the vines are trained to straight sticks like our raspberry-bushes in England.

Q. What country produced the peach?

A. Persia: it was so tender a fruit, that for many years, of all the Roman provinces, it grew no nearer to Rome than Egypt.

Q. But is it not now universal in Europe?

A. Yes: as well as the nectarine,

which is a smooth-skinned variety of peach, but of a richer and more delicious flavour.

Q. Where did the apricot and quince come from?

A. Epirus, Carthage, Armenia, and Syria.

Q. Where is Epirus?

A. It was part of ancient Greece, but now forms a portion of Turkey in Europe.

Q. Where is Carthage?

A. In the north of Africa; Queen Dido founded it: Tunis stands on its ruins.

Q. Where is Armenia?

A. In Asia, near the Euphrates; it is a very fertile country, watered by several fine rivers.

Q. Where is Syria?

A. In Asia: Damascus is the capital.

Q. Is it not supposed that the apricot is a native of Africa?

A. Yes; it appears to have come from thence, through Persia and Greece, to us, with the name of "Apricus," which signifies "sunny."

F 3

Q. What country first furnished us with the gooseberry?

A. Flanders; it is a most useful common fruit.

Q. Whence have we cherries?

A. This well-known fruit formerly grew wild in the woods near Cerasus, in Pontus.

Q. Where is Pontus?

A. On the southern coast of the Black Sea.

Q. Who first brought them to Rome?

A. Lucullus, a Roman general.

Q. And when were they planted in England?

A. In Henry the Eighth's time, about Sittingbourne, in Kent, which is still famous for its cherry orchards.

Q. Who first planted them in Ireland?

A. Sir Walter Raleigh, on his estate at Youghal, where some of his cherry and myrtle trees are still to be seen.

Q. Do not the Swiss distil a strong spirit from the wild black cherry?

A. Yes; called Kirschewasser; and

sell it to the French and Germans at a considerable profit.

Q. Is not the wood and gum also valuable?

A. Yes; the wood is much used by turners and cabinet-makers, and the gum is very nourishing.

Q. What story is related by Hasselquist to prove this?

A. He informs us that during a siege more than one hundred men were kept alive for two months, by putting a little of this gum into their mouths, and letting it dissolve.

Q. Who was Hasselquist?

A. A Swedish botanist and natural historian, born in East Gothland in 1722.

Q. Who is said to have introduced filbert-nuts?

A. Lucullus, who brought them from Pontus into Italy.

Q. After whom was the filbert named?

A. Philibert, the king of France, who caused by art sundry kinds of nuts to be produced.

Q. Where do the sweet chestnuts

come from, which are roasted and eaten in desserts?

A. Spain and France: those which are grown here are a much smaller fruit than what we receive from abroad.

Q. Is not the leaf of the Spanish chestnut very different from the horse chestnut?

A. Yes; the Spanish chestnut has long pointed leaves, with long tapering notches at the edges.

Q. Is there not a celebrated Spanish chestnut-tree at Tortworth, Gloucester-shire?

A. Yes; it was known as a boundary-mark in the reign of King John, and was then supposed to be more than five hundred years old, making its age at this time to exceed eleven hundred years.

Q. What is its diameter?

A. Fifteen feet; it is forty-five feet round, and it still continues to bear fruit.

Q. What are medlars?

A. A native English fruit, having been remarked more than a century ago

to grow wild in the hedges about Min-
shull in Cheshire.

Q. What is their appearance?

A. They look half rotten when brought
to table; for they are placed in moist
bran for a fortnight, to prepare them for
eating.

Q. What is the pomegranate?

A. An apple-shaped fruit, with a thick
rind and a rich scarlet flower, most highly
valued by the Greeks and Romans.

Q. What is its native soil?

A. Africa, especially the neighbourhood of Carthage, but the tree grows
wild in the north of India and in Persia:
there is scarcely a part of it that is not
useful and agreeable to man.

Q. In what way?

A. In the East they mingle the grains
of it in their wine, and use them for
medicine, being much esteemed for their
great astringency; the rind is also much
preferred for tanning the fine Morocco
leather.

Q. Does not Solomon speak of the
wine made from it?

A. Yes; and Persia still makes great quantities of it.

Q. What are cranberries?

A. A small red fruit about the size of a pea, which grows in the fens in the north of England, Lincolnshire, and Cambridgeshire.

Q. Is not the collecting of cranberries a disagreeable employment?

A. Yes; for each berry grows on a separate stalk, and the gathering is damp, dirty work.

Q. What town is famous for them?

A. Longtown, in Cumberland: their rich flavour is generally esteemed.

Q. Are not many brought to this country from North America and Russia?

A. Yes; they are a larger fruit, but not so pleasant.

Q. What use do the inhabitants of Sweden make of this fruit?

A. They use it to clean their silver plate.

Q. What are guavas?

A. The guava is a West Indian fruit,

both delicious and wholesome; it is eaten raw, but it is prepared as a sweet-meat in many ways, particularly in that form called guava jelly.

Q. Whence have we tamarinds?

A. From both the Indies: they make a most delicious preserve.

Q. To what people are we indebted for the use of tamarinds?

A. To the Arabians: in hot climates they are used in making a cooling and agreeable drink.

Q. What are plums?

A. A well-known fruit in England; the *magnum bonum*, or egg plum, the greengage, and many others, all originally came from the wild plum.

Q. What are prunes?

A. French plums dried; they are usually very prettily packed in boxes, and exported from France.

Q. What do you mean by exported?

A. Sent abroad to other nations.

Q. Whence do they principally come?

A. From Brignolles, a town of Provence about thirty miles from Marseilles;

this is one of the most famous places in France for dried plums ; also from Bourdeaux, a rich town in Guienne.

Q. What are raisins?

A. Very ripe grapes, prepared by drying them in the sun.

Q. Where do they come from ?

A. Most of the southern countries of Europe, but chiefly from Spain.

Q. What city produces the finest, called jar-raisins?

A. Damascus, the capital of Syria.

Q. Where is Syria?

A. A noted country in Asia.

Q. What are currants?

A. A small dried grape, anciently grown in the Isthmus of Corinth, whence they obtained the name of Corinths, since corrupted to currants.

Q. Where do they chiefly come from now?

A. Most of the islands in the Archipelago, and from Zante.

Q. Are the natives acquainted with the use we make of them?

A. No ; they imagine we use them in

the dyeing of cloth, and are ignorant of our luxury of Christmas pies and plum-puddings.

Q. What are figs?

A. The rich soft fruit of the fig-tree.

Q. Does it not appear from history, that the fig-tree was much valued by the ancients?

A. Yes; it was the most common and favourite fruit of the ancient Greeks and the peasants of Italy.

Q. How are figs prepared for exportation?

A. They are dried in a furnace, or in the sun, after being dipped in a scalding preparation, made of the ashes of the fig-tree.

Q. Where do they come from?

A. The best from Turkey, Italy, and Spain: the finest are packed in round boxes called drums, or more usually in small oblong boxes.

Q. Was not the wood of the fig-tree much valued by the ancients?

A. Yes; for although of a spongy texture, it is most durable, and on this account was formerly used in eastern countries in coffins for embalmed bodies.

Q. Why were the ancient Egyptians so anxious about preserving their dead?

A. They believed in the immortality of the soul, and thought that by preserving the body from corruption, they were retaining the soul within it till the day of resurrection.

Q. Have not some of the mummy cloths been found most beautifully decorated?

A. Yes; some few are most delicately and richly embroidered; no doubt the result of feminine love and undying affection for some dear departed object; the Egyptian women excelled in this elegant art.

Q. Are there not two remarkable circumstances connected with the natural history of the fig-tree?

A. Yes; that in some climates it produces a *treble* crop of fruit in one year, and that the fruit always precedes the leaves.

Q. What are almonds?

A. A kernel which is contained in a tender shell, with many small holes on the outside.

Q. What countries furnish us with this pleasant nut?

A. France, Spain, Italy, and the Levant; they are packed in casks and boxes.

Q. What is their use?

A. They are eaten with raisins in desserts, also in confectionery, and by pressure they yield a great deal of oil, used in medicine.

Q. Is there not another kind of almond?

A. Yes; it is called the *bitter* almond from its taste, and it is smaller and flatter than the sweet almond.

Q. Are bitter almonds cultivated in England?

A. No; they are imported from Barbary in large quantities, but the best are brought from Provence.

Q. Is the oil of almonds extracted from both kinds?

A. Yes; but it is yielded in greater abundance from the bitter almond.

Q. What are cocoa-nuts?

A. A woody fruit covered with a fibrous husk, growing on a species of palm in most hot climates, with a firm white kernel.

Q. Is it not a most beautiful as well as useful tree?

A. Yes; it grows from forty to sixty feet high, and has no leaves except at the top, which appear like immense feathers, each fourteen feet long.

Q. How does the fruit grow on this curious tree?

A. The nuts hang down from the summit in clusters of a dozen or more together.

Q. Does it not afford food, milk, oil, clothing, and shelter?

A. Yes; the nut is in shape like a filbert, but very much larger; it yields an oil when pressed like almonds, and when fresh, a quantity of milk is found in it.

Q. From what part are cloth, sails, and cordage made?

A. From the fibrous substance which surrounds the nut, and the trunk is made into boats : so that every part of this tree is of use.

Q. What are capers?

A. The unopened flower-bud of a low creeping shrub which grows wild in the south of France and upon the walls of Rome, Sienna, and Florence.

Q. Where is this shrub largely cultivated?

A. Between Marseilles and Toulon, also at Toulon and Majorca.

Q. When do the caper plants begin to flower?

A. Early in May, when women and children are employed to gather the buds throughout the season till the beginning of frost in November.

Q. How are they disposed of?

A. The produce of each day's gathering is thrown into a cask, with the addition of vinegar and a little salt, so as to keep the buds always covered with liquor.

Q. What are they useful for?

A. They are exported in great quantities, being a favourite sauce for boiled mutton, and are sometimes used in medicine.

Q. Whence have we olives?

A. From Italy, Spain, and the southern parts of France.

Q. Are they eaten fresh?

A. No; they are pickled in salt and water.

Q. Are they considered wholesome?

A. Not for persons of delicate habits, on account of the great quantity of oil contained in them.

Q. What is this oil called?

A. Sweet oil, or oil of olives.

Q. What is it used in?

A. Salads and many other things.

Q. What people first exported olive oil in large quantities?

A. The Tuscans, and thus it has also gained the name of Florence oil; but the purest is said to be obtained from about Aix, in France.

Q. What people used the ceremony of washing the feet, and anointing the head with oil, to a guest?

A. The Jews; they also considered it

a remedy against the bite of all venomous reptiles.

Q. Who is said to have been cast into a cauldron of boiling oil at Rome?

A. St. John the Evangelist, by the command of the Emperor Domitian; but instead of destroying him he was not even hurt.

Q. Where was he afterwards banished to?

A. The island of Patmos, where he wrote the Revelation.

Q. Where is Patmos?

A. An island in the Archipelago; St. John died at Ephesus, in Asia Minor.

Q. What is the olive-tree considered as a symbol of?

A. Peace.

Q. Is not olive oil used in medicine?

A. Yes; it is said to be a remedy against the bite of the viper.

Q. Are there not two or three different kinds of oil, which are of great use?

A. Yes.

Q. What is common or train oil?

A. An oil extracted from the fat of whales.

Q. What is this fat called ?

A. Blubber; it is found beneath the skin to the depth of ten or twelve inches.

Q. What is train oil used for ?

A. It is burnt in lamps, and is very useful in cleaning wool, and in other manufactures.

Q. Are there any other sorts of oil?

A. Yes; there is an oil obtained from rape-seed, by pressure.

Q. What is this oil sometimes called?

A. Colza oil, and it has recently come into general use for lamps.

Q. What is rape-seed ?

A. The seed of a kind of cabbage which grows on a rich soil, and is so fine, that they thresh it on a large cloth in the field.

Q. After the oil has been pressed out of it, what is the remainder called ?

A. Oil-cake: it is much used for fattening oxen.

Q. Where does rape-seed grow ?

A. In several parts of England.

Q. What is neat's-foot oil ?

A. It is procured from the feet of

oxen, and is of great use in preparing and softening leather.

Q. What is linseed oil?

A. It is pressed from the seed of flax, and is useful in medicine and the arts.

Q. What is cajeput oil?

A. A beautiful green-coloured oil, produced from the leaves of a tree-shrub growing in the East Indies, highly valued there for many complaints, and used in the preservation of subjects in natural history.

Q. Where is it chiefly prepared?

A. In the island of Bouro, one of the Moluccas, from whence it is imported; but from its high price it is seldom to be had genuine.

Q. Has it not a very powerful smell?

A. Yes; which is remarkably destructive to insects.

Q. What is petroleum?

A. A very inflammable mineral oil recently discovered in many parts of the world.

Q. What is cod-liver oil?

A. An oil extracted from the putrid liver of the cod-fish by exposing it to heat.

Q. For what is it now much used?

A. To give strength to persons in consumption and other debilitating diseases.

Q. Is it not highly valuable when used in this way?

A. Yes: it is perhaps the most efficacious medicine that has been used in England for many years.

Q. Pray which are the most valuable or most common kinds of fish?

A. The salmon, the turbot, the cod, the sole, the mackerel, and the herring.

Q. Where is the salmon caught?

A. Chiefly in the river and frith of Tay, and other rivers and friths of Scotland; it is also found in Ireland, near Limerick and Cork, and in some of the rivers of England.

Q. What is the turbot?

A. A large flat fish, mostly caught off the coasts of Yorkshire and Holland.

Q. Where is the cod-fish caught?

A. Chiefly off the coasts of Newfoundland in North America; the fish are then either dried or salted and barrelled, and sent in large quantities to England and the south of Europe.

Q. But do we not frequently eat fresh cod during December and the following months?

A. Yes; these are generally caught on the Dogger Bank, between England and Holland.

Q. What is the sole?

A. A small flat fish, caught off most parts of our coasts; it is best for eating during the month of June.

Q. What is the mackerel?

A. A small fish caught in great abundance in every part of our coasts in the spring and early part of the summer.

Q. Is there not a peculiarity about it?

A. Yes; it spoils sooner than any kind of fish, and may therefore be sold on Sunday.

Q. Is not the herring the cheapest of all fish?

A. Yes, and by far the most plentiful; they are found in immense floating shoals in many parts of the northern seas.

Q. Is not Yarmouth, in Norfolk, celebrated for its herring fishery?

A. Yes; the great season commences about the end of August, and upwards of seventy tons' weight of this little fish have been captured in one night.

Q. What little fish is caught in abundance in the river Thames between Greenwich and Woolwich?

A. The whitebait, a very small white fish; it is considered a great delicacy.

Q. What is isinglass?

A. A glue made of the sounds and air-bladders of fish.

Q. What fish particularly furnishes isinglass?

A. The sturgeon, found in the river Volga: the Russians long kept the secret of preparing it.

Q. What is it useful for?

A. It is used by brewers and others, for fining and clearing all fermented liquors: also in medicine, and in cookery for making jellies.

Q. Are not vast quantities of sturgeon caught annually in the Caspian Sea?

A. Yes; from 300,000 to 400,000; and from the species called the starred sturgeon, the best caviar and the strongest isinglass are obtained.

Q. What is caviar?

A. A food made from the roes of the sturgeon, much eaten by the Russians.

Q. What is done with all sturgeons caught near London?

A. They are taken to the lord mayor, and by him presented to the sovereign.

Q. What gave rise to this custom?

A. The flesh of the sturgeon was so valued in the time of the Emperor Severus, that it was brought to table by servants with coronets on their heads, preceded by music. Its taste can scarcely be distinguished from veal.

Q. Do not the people of Astrakan dry these sturgeons in the sun, before the doors of their houses?

A. Yes; and the smell of them attracts such prodigious swarms of flies into the city, that the very air seems alive with them.

Q. Where is the Caspian Sea?

A. It is a great lake in Asia; and

besides sturgeon, it has fine salmon and herrings.

Q. Where is Astrakan?

A. A city on the Caspian Sea : rain seldom falls there : but it is situated on the banks of the Volga, which overflows, and when the water retires, the grass grows in less than a month.

Q. What is spermaceti ?

A. It is a white fat substance, found in an immense cavity in the skull of the whale, distinct from the brain.

Q. Is it not a fluid when the animal is alive ?

A. Yes; but when dead it is found in solid lumps of a whitish colour.

Q. Is spermaceti found in all whales?

A. No ; it is the produce of a particular kind of whale called the sperm whale, known from the common whale by having a hunch on its back.

Q. What are the uses of spermaceti?

A. It is of great use in medicine, for coughs and inward bruises: and candles are also made of it.

Q. What are yams ?

A. A certain root used by the Americans for feeding their negroes.

Q. Is it not a singular root in shape ?

A. Yes ; it is very large, and looks like a man's leg.

Q. Are not yams sometimes boiled for food, or ground into flour?

A. Yes.

Q. What are dates ?

A. A fruit shaped like a large acorn, and much eaten by the Africans and Egyptians.

Q. Where is the date or palm-tree principally cultivated ?

A. On the African coast of the Mediterranean, and also in Arabia and Persia.

Q. Are not dates the principal part of the subsistence of the inhabitants of those countries?

A. Yes.

Q. Are not the leaves of this tree very large ?

A. Yes ; they are eight or nine feet long, and are sent to Italy under the name of palms, to be used in the grand religious processions on Palm Sunday.

Q. Which is Palm Sunday?

A. The Sunday before Easter, when the multitude cut down palm-trees and strewed them in the path of our Lord.

Q. What are cucumbers?

A. A cooling fruit, always eaten before it is ripe, with vinegar, oil, pepper, and salt. They are sometimes stewed.

Q. From what country were they brought?

A. From the Levant: they are raised in hot-beds under glass in this country.

Q. What are gherkins?

A. Very young cucumbers pickled with vinegar and spice.

Q. What is the common melon?

A. A species of cucumber. In hot climates this fruit attains great perfection; in ours it is raised under glass.

Q. What is the water melon?

A. Another species highly valued in hot climates for its delicious flavour and coolness. It melts in the mouth, and, like the fluid in the cocoa-nut, may be poured through a hole and drunk.

Q. What countries particularly value them?

A. Egypt, China, and the East Indies; their pulp in general is of a reddish colour.

Q. What are mangoes?

A. Such as we see in this country are the unripe fruit of a large East Indian tree pickled in vinegar.

Q. Is it a fruit much esteemed in India?

A. Yes: when ripe it is about the size of a goose's egg; its smell is so refreshing, that it is thought it will restore persons in a declining state of health.

Q. What are bananas, or plantains?

A. The fruit of a valuable tree much cultivated in the East Indies and other tropical countries; it has a soft stem fifteen or twenty feet high, with a cluster of leaves at the top.

Q. Are not the leaves very large?

A. Yes; they are frequently eight feet long, and more than two broad; the fruit is shaped like a cucumber, and produced in bunches so large as each to weigh forty pounds and upwards.

Q. Is it an agreeable fruit?

A. Yes; for when ripe it is filled with a pulp of luscious sweet taste, and is frequently introduced in desserts in the East Indies.

Q. Is not the fruit usually gathered before it is ripe?

A. Yes; and after the skin has been peeled off, it is roasted for a little while in a clear fire, then scraped and eaten as bread, for which it is an excellent substitute.

Q. Are they not also boiled?

A. Yes; they are also fried, pounded, made into puddings, and used in various ways.

Q. By whom is this tree reckoned invaluable?

A. By the negroes of the West Indian islands, and the wild tribes of South America, who depend upon this fruit for their subsistence.

Q. What are capsicums?

A. South American and Indian plants known by their pods of shining red or yellow colour, which contain many small seeds.

Q. What are they useful for?

A. In hot climates they are eaten in large quantities, both in animal and vegetable food.

Q. What is cayenne-pepper?

A. It is made from the fruit of different species of capsicums.

Q. What process does it undergo?

A. When ripe it is dried in the sun, pounded, and mixed with a certain quantity of salt: then kept for use, closely stopped in bottles.

Q. Is it considered wholesome and useful?

A. Both; for it is much used in eating, and is strongly recommended by doctors in gouty and paralytic cases, to promote the action of the organs when languid.

Q. What is garlic?

A. A bulbous root of an offensive smell and strong flavour, much eaten by the lower classes of the French, Spaniards, and Portuguese.

Q. What other people eat it to excess?

A. The Jews; it is also much used in medicine, in dropsy, asthmas, agues, and all nervous disorders.

Q. Has it not been found of use in curing deafness?

A. Yes; by wrapping a clove of garlic in mustard and putting it into the ear.

Q. Is not the juice of garlic said to be a strong cement?

A. Yes; the strongest that can be used for broken glass or china.

Q. Where does this plant grow wild?

A. In the island of Sicily.

Q. What are leeks?

A. A bulbous root of the garlic tribe, much used in some countries, in soups, broths, &c.

Q. What country are they natives of?

A. Switzerland.

Q. What nation wear the leek as a badge of honour?

A. The Welsh, on the 1st of March, the day of their patron saint, St. David.

Q. What gave rise to this curious custom?

A. It happened that during the Welsh wars, a party of Welshmen wanted a mark of distinction, and, passing through a field of leeks, they seized and stuck the plants in their caps, and under this signal they were victorious.

Q. What is the Canadian, or tree-onion?

A. A curious plant, which produces its onions on the top of the stalk.

Q. What are shalots?

A. A kind of garlic, much used by the French in cookery.

Q. What is soy?

A. A dark-coloured sauce, made from the seeds of a Chinese bean.

Q. Is there not a joke among seamen, that soy is made from beetles and cockroaches?

A. Yes; it originates from a fancied resemblance in the colour and shape of the seeds to the beetle.

Q. Where is this esteemed sauce prepared?

A. Chiefly in China and Japan; that brought from the latter place is usually preferred.

Q. What is the anchovy?

A. A small fish of the herring tribe, made into a well-known sauce, or salted and pickled.

Q. Where are anchovies caught?

A. In the Mediterranean; but the principal fishery is on the shores of Gorgona, a small island near Leghorn, in Italy.

Q. What is ketchup?

A. A well-known sauce made from the common mushroom.

Q. What are mushrooms?

A. A fungus found wild in parks and pastures, where the turf has not been ploughed for many years.

Q. What are morels?

A. A kind of fungus found in woods and hedges, used for thickening and heightening the flavour of sauces and soups.

Q. How are they preserved?

A. They are strung upon packthread and dried.

Q. What is saloop?

A. A nourishing drink sold very early

in the morning in the streets of London to the poor.

Q. What is it made of?

A. An infusion of sassafras mixed with milk, which is considered very nourishing.

Q. Who value this drink highly?

A. The Turks; what we use in this country is principally prepared and brought from the Levant.

Q. What is sassafras?

A. The wood, root, and bark of a species of laurel-tree growing in North America, used in medicine.

Q. Has it not a very powerful scent, disagreeable to insects?

A. Yes; therefore in America they make bed-posts of the wood, and put it into wardrobes to prevent moths.

Q. What is common salt?

A. A preparation extracted from sea-water and brine springs.

Q. How is this done?

A. By putting sea-water into large shallow leaden troughs, from which the water is evaporated by means of fire, and the salt is found at the bottom.

Q. Of what use is salt?

A. It is used in cookery, in preserving food, in agriculture, and in many other ways; soda and other valuable products are obtained from it.

Q. Is there any other kind of salt?

A. Yes; there is a finer sort, called rock-salt, that is dug out of mines.

Q. Where are these mines?

A. In several places; but the most noted one is at Wielitska, near Cracow, in Poland.

Q. Is there not something very remarkable about this mine?

A. Yes; it is inhabited, and there are houses, chapels, and streets of rock-salt formed in it.

Q. Is it not extremely beautiful?

A. Yes; and when illuminated it sparkles like diamonds.

Q. To whom does this mine belong?

A. To the Emperor of Austria: it has been worked since the year 1251, and affords support to many thousands; it must be well worth viewing.

Q. Are there not salt-mines in England?

A. Yes; at Northwich and Nantwich, and other places in Cheshire, there are salt-mines of great depth and extent, frequently visited by travellers.

Q. Are there not also mountains of salt?

A. Yes; there is one five hundred feet high, near Cardona, fifty miles from Barcelona, in Spain; also one in Lahore, a province of Hindostan; and in Peru.

Q. You said salt is also obtained from brine springs: are there any in England?

A. Yes; the principal ones are at Droitwich, in Worcestershire; they are four in number.

Q. Where is salt considered very valuable?

A. In Abyssinia, where every person who can carries a small piece of it suspended in a bag from his girdle.

Q. For what purpose is this odd custom observed?

A. The heat of the climate renders the mouth parched and dried; and

H

when two friends meet, they produce their bit of salt, and give it to each other to lick, as a mark of civility and friendship.

Q. Is it then so great a luxury?

A. Yes; Mungo Park tells us that, in the interior of Africa, to say, "A man eats salt with his provisions," is the same as saying, "*He is a rich man.*"

Q. Was it not the practice in England in the middle ages to place a large salt-cellar in the centre of the dinner-table?

A. Yes: and it was considered honourable to sit above the salt, the domestics and inferior guests sitting at the lower end of the table below it.

Q. Did the family and their servants take their meals at the same table?

A. It was in those times the custom to do so.

Q. What is bay-salt?

A. That which is produced from the evaporation of sea-water by the heat of the sun only.

Q. What is saltpetre?

A. It is another sort of salt, found

pure on the surface of the earth in some parts of India, Africa, and Spain, where it is swept off at certain seasons twice or three times a week.

Q. But is it not artificially made?

A. Yes; from the refuse of animal and vegetable substances, which undergo a state of putrefaction.

Q. From what country does it chiefly come?

A. The East Indies; the quantity annually brought to this country from the Presidency of Bengal is now about 250,000 cwt.

Q. What other name is saltpetre also known by?

A. That of nitre.

Q. What renders it of so much importance?

A. Its being a principal ingredient in the composition of that destructive article called gunpowder.

Q. What is gunpowder?

A. A mixture of nitre, sulphur, and charcoal; but by far the greatest part is nitre.

Q. How was gunpowder invented?

A. A monk of Cologne, called Swartz, when making chemical experiments, discovered that the above mixture, finely powdered, would produce an explosive quality.

Q. But who discovered its great and destructive powers?

A. Roger Bacon, a learned English monk, in the reign of Edward I.; he spoke of it as a potent engine in the destruction of armies.

Q. When was it first used in battle?

A. At Cressy, and afterwards at the siege of Calais.

Q. Is it not said that the Chinese were acquainted with gunpowder long before this period?

A. Yes.

Q. What other delightful discoveries did Roger Bacon make?

A. He invented reading glasses, and many useful mathematical instruments.

Q. Did he not also invent telescopes and microscopes?

A. He appears to have been aware that lenses or glasses might be so arranged as to magnify objects ; but the merit of having first made telescopes of any practical use appears to belong to Galileo, an Italian.

Q. Is Bacon not also said to have made the first map ?

A. Yes ; it was one of the country of Tartary : he formed it from the description he obtained from some travellers.

Q. Was he not looked upon as a magician in those ignorant days ?

A. Yes ; and was thrown into prison, where he was kept several years : he died a very old man at Oxford.

Q. What is common sulphur, or brimstone ?

A. It is a yellow, dry substance, which in burning yields a suffocating fume.

Q. Whence do we have it ?

A. It is dug out of the earth in many places, particularly in Sicily, Italy, Switzerland, and South America.

Q. What is aqua-fortis ?

A. A mixture of nitre and clay distilled in a glass apparatus.

Q. What is the great use of aqua-fortis?

A. All metals except gold and platina can be dissolved in it.

Q. What great use do dyers make of it?

A. They use it for dissolving tin, and forming, with madder, that beautiful scarlet colour so much admired.

Q. Was not this great secret discovered to the English by chance?

A. Yes; a girl at an inn wanted to dye some ribbons, and asked her lover, who worked at a manufactory, for a little scarlet dye.

Q. What did she do with it?

A. She put it into one of the porter pots, and, having nothing better, she boiled her ribbons in it, and they came out a most brilliant colour.

Q. Was not her lover surprised when he saw it?

A. Exceedingly so, and being a clever fellow, he imagined the tin pot had caused it, and by this means discovered an important secret.

Q. What is madder?

A. A trailing plant much cultivated in Holland, France, and Italy, on account of its roots, which are used by dyers and calico-printers.

Q. What colour is procured from it?

A. A fine red colour; and it also forms a first tint for various other shades.

Q. What other foreign countries produce it?

A. It grows wild in South America, and in the neighbourhood of Smyrna; and the island of Cyprus produces a kind which affords a very beautiful colour.

Q. What animals are very fond of madder?

A. Cows; it makes their butter of a fine yellow colour.

Q. What are wafers?

A. They are made of flour, isinglass, and a small quantity of yeast.

Q. What more is done?

A. This mixture is coloured, spread

out in very thin cakes on tin plates, dried on a stove, and cut into wafers.

Q. What is ink?

A. A mixture of galls, copperas, gum-arabic, and water.

Q. What are galls?

A. A swelling on the leaves of the oak, occasioned by the bite of small insects, which lodge their eggs in it.

Q. Are galls useful?

A. Yes; quantities of them are used in dyeing and for other purposes.

Q. What is copperas?

A. A mineral salt formed from iron and sulphuric acid, produced by the moisture of the atmosphere.

Q. What is its colour?

A. A bright green; it is in much request by dyers, tanners, and the manufacturers of ink.

Q. What is red ink?

A. It is made by mixing a decoction of Brazil wood with alum and gum-water, in lieu of galls, &c.

Q. Pray are our inks equal to those of antiquity?

A. No; they are very inferior, as is proved by rolls and records of the seventeenth century; which are scarcely legible, while some Saxon manuscripts, written in England, exceed in colour any thing of the kind.

Q. What is gum-arabic?

A. A well-known drug, the sap of a tree which grows in Egypt, Turkey, and in the neighbourhood of the Persian Gulf; it issues from the bark like the gum of the cherry and plum tree.

Q. Is gum-arabic a useful drug?

A. Yes; it was formerly much used in medicine, but now it is principally in request by dyers and the manufacturers of water colours, &c.

Q. Is it not also a useful cement?

A. Yes; dissolved in white vinegar it makes a very delicate one for card-work, &c.

Q. But will not common vinegar answer the same purpose?

A. Yes; except as to colour; and in both cases, if kept corked, it will not dry up.

Q. What is pounce, or gum-sandarach?

A. The gum of the common juniper; when powdered and passed through a fine sieve, it is called pounce, and used upon writing paper when it has been scratched.

Q. By whom is gum-sandarach much used?

A. By cabinet-makers and painters, in the preparation of varnish.

Q. What is paper made of?

A. Linen and cotton rags; an inferior kind is made from straw and other fibrous substances.

Q. What do the Chinese make it of?

A. Silk.

Q. Are not some coloured rags bleached white for the purpose of making common writing paper?

A. Yes; but the superfine writing paper is made of white rags.

Q. How is paper made?

A. The rags are first sorted; the white ones make writing paper, and the coloured ones are used for the commoner sorts.

Q. What is then done?

A. They are carried to a mill, and put into an engine placed in clean water.

Q. What sort of an engine is it?

A. It is an iron instrument with long sharp teeth, or knives, which, by moving round very quickly, soon tears the rags asunder, and reduces them to a pulp.

Q. What is next done?

A. This pulp is put into a copper of warm water, and then resembles thin starch, and moulds of the size of a sheet of paper are dipped into it.

Q. What are these moulds like?

A. A frame with a most delicately fine wire net.

Q. What is next done?

A. The paper is made by gently shaking this mould when dipped in the pulp till it is as thick as it is wanted.

Q. How do they then proceed?

A. Each sheet is then placed between two pieces of woollen cloth, and taken directly to be pressed, after which it is taken out and hung up separately to dry : it is then sized.

Q. Why is paper sized?

A. To prevent the ink sinking into the paper and spreading: before it is sized it is blotting paper.

Q. What is size?

A. A kind of glue.

Q. How is it made?

A. From the parings which are cut off the edges of sheep-skins, and also from slips of parchment: the size made from the latter is the best.

Q. Will not nearly all this labour soon be given up?

A. Yes; for a very curious machine has been invented some time, and is now brought to great perfection, which converts the pulp into a finished sheet of paper in a few minutes.

Q. But is not the best writing paper still made by hand, as above described?

A. Yes.

Q. Was paper known to the ancients?

A. Not such as we use; the Egyptians prepared a rush called papyrus, whence the word paper is derived.

Q. Where did this rush grow?

A. Principally about the banks of the Nile, in Egypt.

Q. Who is said to have been exposed in a basket made of these rushes?

A. Moses : and the inhabitants even now weave it into cloth, mattresses, ropes, &c.

Q. Where was the first paper-mill erected in England?

A. At Dartford, in Kent, in 1588, by Sir John Spielman, a German, who was knighted by Queen Elizabeth.

Q. But is not this common opinion now questioned?

A. Yes; for Shakspeare, in his play of Henry VI., mentions paper-mills, so that they must have existed in this country before the time of Spielman, although he probably introduced improvements in the manufacture.

Q. Who brought the art of paper-making to any perfection?

A. One Thomas Watkins, a stationer, in 1713; and to the industry of this individual we owe the origin of our numerous paper-mills.

Q. Was not the use of paper known in the time of Harold?

A. Yes; but England was slow in adopting the art as a manufacture of her own.

Q. How long have paper-hangings been in use?

A. About two centuries; in the middle ages the walls were covered with tapestry, but it was too expensive for common use.

Q. What methods are adopted in producing the required device?

A. A block is carved for each colour, and an impression is taken upon the paper from each block in succession.

Q. Has not a more expeditious method been recently invented?

A. Yes; cheap papers are now printed by means of a revolving cylinder, which produces all the colours at once.

Q. How many yards will one of these machines print in a day?

A. Upwards of 18,000, and the pattern is printed upon the paper in lengths of half a mile.

Q. Are they not then divided?

A. Yes; into lengths of twelve yards.

Q. What is *papier mâché?*

A. A preparation of moistened paper of considerable thickness, which is made into tea-trays, dressing-cases, portfolios, and other articles of great beauty.

Q. How is it made?

A. There are two sorts; the commoner kind is made by pasting together several sheets of prepared paper, the better sort by converting the paper into pulp and pressing it into moulds.

Q. What are pens?

A. The pen is an instrument to write with, made of quills taken from the wings of ravens, turkeys, peacocks, and geese.

Q. What poor bird is stripped whilst alive, every year, for the sake of its quills, or large feathers in the wings?

A. The goose: great numbers of them are kept in the fens of Lincolnshire for this purpose.

Q. Are they not also tormented for

the down, or small feathers, which grow under the wing?

A. Yes; occasionally five times a year they undergo this painful operation, for the purpose of stuffing our beds, bolsters, and pillows.

Q. What glorious event is by some supposed to be commemorated by eating goose on Michaelmas-day?

A. The defeat of the Spanish Armada. Queen Elizabeth was at dinner when the news was brought her, and she commanded that the dish (a goose) then before her might be served up every Michaelmas-day.

Q. But is it not now the prevailing opinion that this custom is of more ancient date?

A. Yes.

Q. Who write with reeds to this day?

A. The Turks, Moors, and Eastern people.

Q. What did the ancients use?

A. An iron style; it was sharp at one end, like a needle, to write with, and at the other end blunt and broad to scratch out with.

Q. Upon what did they write with these iron styles?

A. Upon waxen tablets: but for writing upon papyrus, or parchment, they used reeds.

Q. Who has humorously remarked that the goose, the bee, and the calf rule the world?

A. Mr. Howell; the first furnishing quills; the second, wax; and the last, parchment.

Q. What ingenious invention has in a great measure superseded the use of quills?

A. The invention of the steel pen in Birmingham.

Q. How many pairs of hands are constantly employed in the manufacture of this article?

A. Some thousands; and it consumes several hundred tons of steel per annum.

Q. How many pens will one ton of steel produce?

A. Nearly two millions ; great quantities of them are exported : each pen passes through fourteen stages before it is finished.

Q. What foreign countries supply us with quills ?

A. Polish Prussia, and they are also imported from Russia.

Q. By whom was the first post-office set up in England ?

A. By Charles I.; he appointed a post to carry letters once a week between London and Edinburgh.

Q. Who greatly extended this benefit ?

A. Oliver Cromwell.

Q. Has not the business of the post-office been very much extended of late years ?

A. Yes ; since 1840, when the rate of postage was reduced to an uniform charge of one penny.

Q. What has been the result ?

A. At the present time upwards of six hundred millions of letters pass through the post-office every year : this appears by the Postmaster-General's report to be about six times the number under the former system.

Q. What is pasteboard?

A. A card formed of several sheets of paper pasted together and pressed.

Q. What is parchment?

A. The skin of sheep and goats, prepared by softening the skins in lime-pits, and then rendering them fit for writing by the process of rubbing pounded chalk well into the moistened surface with pumice-stone.

Q. Who is said to have been the inventor?

A. Eumenes, king of Pergamus; but he was the improver rather than the inventor of parchment.

Q. Why is this supposed?

A. Because the Persians and others are said to have written all their records on skins long before the time of Eumenes; but Ptolemy, king of Egypt, refusing to supply him with the papyrus rush, he turned his attention to the preparation of the skins of animals as a substitute.

Q. Were not the ancients very curious in having their manuscripts richly ornamented ?

A. Yes; their tablets were adorned with gold borders, and besides the tint of purple with which they tinged their vellum, and the liquid gold used for their ink, they inlaid their covers with precious stones.

Q. Which were the two most valuable libraries among the ancients ?

A. That of Alexandria, collected by the Ptolemies, kings of Egypt, and the other at Pergamus, collected by Eumenes. Mark Antony gave the latter to Cleopatra, and these valuable collections were then united, and most unfortunately lost by being burnt by the Saracens in the year 642.

Q. What is vellum ?

A. The skin of young calves: it is finer, whiter, and smoother than common parchment.

Q. To what purposes are vellum and parchment now principally applied ?

A. For writing deeds upon, as being

more durable than paper; the lawyers use great quantities of it.

Q. Where is it principally prepared?

A. In France.

Q. What is sealing-wax?

A. It is made of shell-lac, cinnabar, and Venetian turpentine, which are melted, prepared, and coloured with vermilion, according to fancy.

Q. What is shell-lac?

A. A substance left by an insect on many trees in the East Indies.

Q. What is cinnabar?

A. A red ore from which mercury is chiefly obtained.

Q. Where are there large mines of it?

A. At Almaden in Spain, also in Hungary and Transylvania.

Q. What is India-rubber?

A. The dried juice of a large tree called the syringe-tree, growing in Guiana, Quito, Cayenne, and other parts of South America.

Q. Does it not rank as one of the most magnificent forest trees?

A. Undoubtedly; for it is second

only to the banian-tree, and may be distinguished at a distance of several miles by its dense, immense, and lofty crown, being 100 feet high, and its branches extend over a very considerable area.

Q. How is the juice procured?

A. By transverse incisions made in the bark; under the incision a hole is scooped out in the earth, in which a leaf folded up in the shape of a rude cup is placed to catch it.

Q. What is the colour of the fluid?

A. When good, of a very fine white colour, about the consistence of cream; it flows rapidly at first during the night, but in two or three days it forms a layer over the wound, and ceases.

Q. How is it converted into the state in which we use it?

A. The juice is spread over moulds prepared for the purpose.

Q. What is then done?

A. These moulds are hung over smoke till quite dry, when they are broken to pieces, and the rubber is fit for use.

Q. What use do the Indians make of it ?

A. They make flambeaux: also boots, bottles, and a kind of cloth, all of which are impenetrable to the water.

Q. What use do we make of it ?

A. It was for a long time simply used in drawing, to efface the marks of black-lead pencils; but within the last few years it has been formed into a variety of articles.

Q. How has this been effected ?

A. After various experiments, it has been discovered how to dissolve this substance, without its losing its elasticity.

Q. What do you mean by elasticity ?

A. It is that property in bodies, by which, on being bent or pressed, they spring back into their natural form.

Q. What has been found the best solvent yet discovered ?

A. Ether, essential oil of coal-tar, naphtha, and oil of sassafras.

Q. How is it used when in a dissolved state ?

A. Thin layers of the dissolved rubber

are spread on cloth, over which another prepared in the same way is laid, and then they are pressed together ; and of this cloth cloaks, bags, cushions, and a variety of waterproof articles are manufactured.

Q. Are not ingenious men daily making discoveries in the application of this useful article ?

A. Yes ; for whale-lines, cables, horse-girths, and surgical bandages are now prepared with it.

Q. Has not an oil been extracted from it for lamps ?

A. Yes : by distillation it yields a fine brilliant light equal to gas, without its offensive smell.

Q. Has not a process been recently invented, whereby elastic India-rubber may be made perfectly solid ?

A. Yes ; after undergoing a certain preparation, it is subjected to the pressure of steam, and thereby becomes hard and brittle, although difficult to break.

Q. For what is it then used ?

A. For hair-combs, and in many kinds of cabinet work it is a good subtitute for ebony.

Q. When was it known in Europe?

A. Not till 1770, when Dr. Priestley ecommended it to those who practised lrawing.

Q. Has not the use of India-rubber)een in some measure superseded by a ·ecent discovery?

A. Yes: many articles formerly made)f that substance are now made of gutta)ercha.

Q. What is gutta percha?

A. The dried sap of a tree, growng in the islands of Singapore and 3orneo.

Q. Where are those islands?

A. In Asia: off the eastern coast of Hindostan.

Q. Who introduced gutta percha to :he attention of this country?

A. Dr. Montgomerie, in 1843.

Q. Is the tree from which gutta)ercha is obtained a large one?

A. Yes; it is often six feet in dia-

meter : its wood is of no use as timber.

Q. How is the sap obtained?

A. By cutting notches in the bark,
from which a milky juice exudes, which
very soon curdles.

Q. For what purpose is gutta percha
applied?

A. To make the soles of boots and
shoes, picture-frames, surgical bandages,
traces, tubing, and many other things,
and also to render cloths, &c., waterproof.

Q. What are the chief properties of
gutta percha?

A. It is not affected by cold or damp :
it may be softened by dipping it in hot
water, when it may be made into any
shape : it is of a strongly adhesive nature,
and is free from the stickiness found in
India-rubber.

Q. Are not pencils made from black
lead?

A. No; they are very improperly so
called, being composed of a very rare
compound mineral substance, which is
called by the scientific *plumbago*, but

by the miners *wadd :* it is of a soft and greasy nature, found in masses or lumps from three to four lbs. each, between layers of slate.

Q. Where is the finest mine in the world for this material?

A. At Borrowdale, in Cumberland: its produce is so valuable that it was only opened once in from four to seven years, and in one hour a single workman could obtain two thousand pounds' worth. After a sufficient quantity has been obtained, it is carefully secured and shut up again.

Q. But has it not recently been found necessary to open this mine every year?

A. Yes; and it is to be feared that the supply will soon entirely fail.

Q. Does the plumbago undergo any process before it is made into pencils?

A. Yes; it is boiled in oil, to render it fit for being sawn into very thin square slips, which are inserted into a little hollow groove, cut in one piece of cedar, over which another is glued.

Q. Is this the only one known?

A. It was thought so; a few other mines have lately been discovered, but the lead is very inferior, being gritty and hard: English drawing-pencils of the best quality are so sought after, that hundreds of thousands are yearly made for exportation.

Q. What is glue?

A. It is made from the skin and sinews of animals boiled down to a strong jelly.

Q. How are painting-brushes made?

A. By filling quills with camels' hair.

Q. What is remarkable of the hair of the camel?

A. Its softness and fineness; so that it is manufactured into the beautiful shawls so much valued from India.

Q. What do they use for other brushes?

A. Hogs' bristles; and they are also used by shoemakers in the place of needles.

Q. What is sponge?

A. It is said to be formed by an

animal which remains fixed on the rocks covered with sea-water.

Q. Is not the growth of sponge very rapid?

A. Yes; it is often found in perfection on rocks, from which only two years before it had been entirely cleared.

Q. From whence is it generally brought?

A. From Constantinople, the States of Barbary, and the islands in the Archipelago.

Q. Where is Constantinople?

A. In European Turkey, of which it is the capital.

Q. Where are the States of Barbary?

A. In the north of Africa.

Q. What is sponge valued for?

A. Its use in surgery; and in painting, to wash out or soften colours; and also for domestic purposes.

Q. What is cork?

A. The bark of a beautiful tree, which is a kind of large green oak.

Q. Where does it grow?

A. In Italy, Spain, Portugal, and

most of the southern countries of
Europe.

Q. Does not the removal of the bark
injure the tree?

A. No; for the cork is really dead
bark, and when the tree is about fifteen
years old it is fit to be barked, which
cannot be done oftener than every eight
or ten years.

Q. Is it prepared in any way?

A. It is soaked in water, and dried
over a strong fire.

Q. What use is made of cork?

A. Principally to stop bottles, to
make floats for nets, buoys for rivers
to direct vessels, for soles of shoes, and
jackets to swim in.

Q. Did not the Egyptians make their
coffins of cork?

A. Yes; and lined them with a resinous composition, to preserve their embalmed bodies.

Q. What is Spanish black, so much
used by printers?

A. Burnt cork; the parings are generally sold for this purpose.

Q. From what are candles principally made ?

A. From tallow.

Q. What is tallow ?

A. The fat of sheep and oxen.

Q. What is done with the fat to prepare it ?

A. It is melted in water, boiled several times, and cleared by the addition of alum.

Q. How are mould-candles made ?

A. By pouring melted tallow into pewter moulds, in the middle of which a cotton has been fixed.

Q. How do they make the kitchen candles ?

A. By tying the wicks on a long stick, and then dipping them two or three times in hot melted tallow, until the candles become of a proper size.

Q. In which of our kings' reigns were tallow candles considered a great luxury ?

A. In Henry the Third's time ; splinters of wood being then burnt in common.

Q. Which of our early kings used to count time by means of candles?

A. Alfred the Great, who had candles made which were painted in rings and belts of different breadths and colours.

Q. For what purpose?

A. He knew by the burning of these candles when he had been employed long enough about any one thing.

Q. Did this clever invention quite answer his purpose?

A. No; for he found when the wind blew upon them they burnt quicker, and this led him to contrive lanterns to put them in.

Q. Is there not a splendid festival held in China, called the feast of lanterns?

A. Yes; on the fifteenth day after the commencement of their new year, when such a profusion of rich transparent lanterns are hung out of the houses, that to a stranger the whole empire looks like Fairy-land.

Q. Do not all ranks contribute to this national show?

A. Yes; even the grandees retrench daily and reduce the expenses of their table, equipage, and dress, in order that they may spend more on their lanterns, some of which cost two thousand crowns.

Q. Has it not hitherto been almost impossible for Europeans to visit the interior of China?

A. Yes; for the people refused to have any intercourse with foreigners except at a few sea-ports where tea and other commodities were exported, and travellers into the interior incurred great peril.

Q. Who succeeded in putting an end to this system of exclusion?

A. Lord Elgin, at the end of the Chinese war in 1858; and by treaty we are now authorized to travel in all parts of the empire.

Q. How are rush-lights made?

A. In the same manner as kitchen candles, only the wicks are made of dried peeled rushes.

Q. Is there not a tree called the tallow-tree?

A. Yes; it is a native of China: the fruit of this tree is enclosed in a husk like that of the chestnut, and consists of three white kernels.

Q. How do the Chinese prepare candles from these?

A. They melt the kernels, and add a little oil, and colour them with vermilion: they are better than our tallow candles, but inferior to wax.

Q. How do they form the wick?

A. Of little slips of dry wood, with the pith of a rush entwined round them.

Q. How are wax-candles made?

A. Of melted wax instead of tallow, and they have a flaxen wick, which never wants snuffing.

Q. What are tapers?

A. They are wax-candles made of different sizes, burnt at funeral processions and other Church solemnities.

Q. At whose tomb were tapers kept burning, day and night, for nearly one hundred years?

A. At Henry the Fifth's; but all these

customs were abolished at the Reformation.

Q. What is wax?

A. It is a substance of which the bee forms its comb, of a yellow colour like honey.

Q. What is white wax?

A. It is prepared by melting bees'-wax in water and bleaching it in the sun and air.

Q. What is flax?

A. The produce of a beautiful grass-like annual plant, with slender stalks, small leaves, and blue blossoms.

Q. Where is it grown?

A. In many parts of Great Britain and Ireland; also in Russia, Holland, and Flanders, and other parts of the world.

Q. What is its use?

A. To weave into linen for shirts, sheets, cambric, and many other things.

Q. How is it procured?

A. It is sown in March and April; when ripe it is pulled up by the roots, steeped in water, and by the fermentation which takes place the bark or flaxy substance becomes separated.

Q. Is it necessary to do any thing else?

A. Yes; these threads must be properly dressed and spun according to the purposes for which they are to be used, then woven into linen, after which it must be bleached.

Q. What is bleaching?

A. The method of making linen white, by exposing it to the sun and air; as when it comes from the weaver's hands it is of the colour of flax, which is of a light brown.

Q. How is this operation performed?

A. It is first steeped in bran and water, then well washed, and spread on the grass to dry.

Q. What is next done?

A. Buckets full of water, mixed with a strong ley made of wood ashes, are constantly thrown over it, and the washing and spreading to dry must be often repeated.

Q. Was not linen formerly often steeped in butter-milk?

A. Yes; after which it was well rinsed, and frequently washed in soap

and water, when it became delicately
white.

Q. Has not this tedious process been
materially shortened?

A. Yes; by the substitution of chlorine
or the fumes of sulphur for butter-milk.

Q. What is chlorine?

A. A greenish gas of powerful odour;
it soon destroys any colour.

Q. What places are noted for the
manufacture of flax into linen?

A. The province of Ulster in Ireland,
the towns of Dundee and Glasgow in
Scotland, and the manufacturing districts in Yorkshire and Lancashire.

Q. To what country are we indebted
for this valuable flax plant?

A. It is supposed it came from those
parts of Egypt annually inundated by
the Nile.

Q. Is not this most probable, from
the Egyptians being famous for their
linen?

A. Yes; for many specimens of it
still exist: the yarn was all spun by the
hand, in which they had attained such

K

perfection, that some of the linen made from it was so exquisitely fine as to be called " woven air."

Q. What is recorded by historians to corroborate this fact ?

A. That some of their nets were composed of threads so delicate, that they would pass through a man's ring, and one person could carry a sufficient number to surround a whole wood.

Q. Are we not also told in the history of needlework by the Countess of Wilton, that this fine linen was curiously embellished with rich embroidery?

A. Yes; figures of animals in gold thread were worked with a needle on it, and frequently the gold thread was woven with the linen. The making of a single shirt would frequently cost 10l.

Q. Which of the British Isles is famous for its linen?

A. Ireland : a colony of Scots, in the reign of James I., fled from persecution in their own country, and settled at Coleraine, in Londonderry.

Q. Is it not the principal manufacture of that country?

A. Yes; and flax is cultivated there with great care and success.

Q. Is not Irish cloth used for body-linen by all who can afford it?

A. Yes; it is made of flax, and called Irish linen; and the towns of Belfast, Carrickfergus, and Londonderry, in the north of Ireland, manufacture this article in great perfection.

Q. What is gauze?

A. A thin transparent stuff made of thread or silk; it is striped and figured, and forms a delicate article for trimmings.

Q. What people embroider this delicate material most exquisitely in gold thread?

A. The Turks and Georgians.

Q. What is cambric?

A. The finest of all cloth made of flax: it takes its name from Cambray, where it was first manufactured.

Q. Where is Cambray?

A. A strong fortified town in France, seated on the river Scheldt; in its old

K 2

cathedral, the celebrated Fénélon, who wrote Telemachus, is buried.

Q. What is lawn?

A. A thinner sort of cambric, first brought to England in Elizabeth's reign in very small quantities, used by the wealthy for ruffs.

Q. How does Stow speak of this delicate material?

A. As a "strange and wonderful stuff," which gave rise to a scoff or by-word, that shortly they would wear ruffs of a spider's web.

Q. What difficulty arose from making them of this thin material?

A. The want of some one to starch or stiffen them; nobody could be found in England; but a Dutch woman, of the name of Dinghen, possessed of that knowledge, came to London, and was the first that ever taught starching in this country.

Q. What is damask?

A. A beautiful silk or linen, with large flowers wrought or worked into patterns upon it, invented at Damascus, in Syria, from which place it derives its name.

Q. What places now excel in this manufacture?

A. Tournay in Flanders, and Chalons in Champagne: and it has of late years been brought to wonderful perfection in this country.

Q. Is Damascus famous for any thing else?

A. Yes; it is celebrated for its fine cabinet work, and rich and highly-finished saddles and bridles; the manufacture of Damascus blades, once so famous, no longer exists.

Q. What is damasceening?

A. Cutting steel into different figures, and filling them up with gold and silver wire; it is done for adorning sword-blades, locks of pistols, &c.

Q. What is hemp?

A. The fibrous parts of the stalks of a most useful plant, something like the common nettle.

Q. What is its use?

A. The finer parts, after being pre-

K 3

pared like flax, are spun into thread, and woven into canvas and strong cloth.

Q. Is not canvas an article of the first importance?

A. Yes; for we should have no sails to our ships without it, it being a very stout material woven in England and Scotland for that purpose.

Q. Are there not six or seven different qualities of it?

A. Yes; according to the size or position of the sail to be made.

Q. How many yards does the mainsail of an East Indiaman contain?

. A. Nearly seven hundred yards of canvas: the whole suit of sails for a large ship is about forty in number, and requires as much as 9000 yards.

Q. What else is manufactured from hemp?

A. Twine, ropes, cable, and cordage, of every description.

Q. What is the refuse called?

A. Tow; it was formerly used for lighting matches for cannon, and stopping blood from wounds in battle; its chief use at present is to remove oil from machinery.

Q. What country carries on a great commerce in hemp?

A. The greater part of our hemp comes from Russia; but it is cultivated in Suffolk and Norfolk.

Q. Did not the ancients expend large sums upon the embroidery of their sails?

A. Yes; but their vessels were mere pleasure-boats, built to float upon their rivers during their sacred festivals, or on state occasions, like the barge of Cleopatra, on the river Cydnus, when she went to meet Mark Antony.

Q. What is cotton?

A. A downy substance contained in a pod, which, when ripe, bursts, and the snow-white or yellowish contents are collected.

Q. Where does this plant grow?

A. The very finest comes from the East and West Indies; but until the civil war by far the largest quantity was grown in the United States; it is raised annually from seed, and grows to a considerable height.

Q. Whence do we now obtain our chief supply?

A. From India, Egypt, and Australia.

Q. Are there not two kinds of cotton cultivated in the United States?

A. Yes; a very fine quality, called sea island cotton, grows along the sandy shores of South Carolina, Georgia, &c.: but it can only be produced in limited quantities.

Q. What is the other kind?

A. The upland cotton, of inferior quality; it is separated from the pods by powerful machinery.

Q. How is it sown?

A. On ploughed lands in spring.

Q. What quantity of cotton was imported into Great Britain in 1845?

A. Seven hundred and twenty millions of pounds' weight.

Q. What quantity was imported in the year 1805?

A. About sixty millions of pounds;

probably not more than one-twenty-fifth of the present supply.

Q. Is there not another species of cotton produced from a shrub?

A. Yes; it grows from four to six feet high, and does not last more than six years in bearing.

Q. Does it not produce two varieties?

A. Yes; in the one the cotton is extremely white, in the other it is of a yellowish brown.

Q. What stuff is manufactured from this last sort?

A. Nankeen.

Q. Are there not also cotton-trees?

A. Yes; two sorts grow in Egypt, and arrive at a great size.

Q. What articles are made of this useful plant?

A. Calicoes and muslins, dimities, and many other stuffs.

Q. What is muslin?

A. A fine, thin, transparent texture, made wholly of cotton.

Q. Where did this beautiful manufacture originally come from?

A. The East Indies, chiefly from Bengal; and Dacca, in that province, has long been famous for a superior sort.

Q. Are the East India muslins as much valued as they used to be?

A. No; for muslins are now made equally fine at Glasgow and Paisley.

Q. Where are these two towns?

A. In the counties of Lanark and Renfrew in Scotland.

Q. What is crape?

A. A thin stuff of silk loosely woven, invented at Bologna, in Italy.

Q. What is camlet or camelot?

A. A stuff made chiefly of goats' hair.

Q. From what are the fine Cashmere shawls made?

A. From the delicate wool of a species of goat found in Thibet and Cashmere, on the borders of the Himalaya mountains, also in Tartary.

Q. Are they not highly prized?

A. Yes; and were so expensive that some have been known to fetch two or three hundred guineas each: very costly shawls are also made from the wool of the broad-tail sheep, a native of Tartary, Thibet, and Persia.

Q. Is not the operation extremely slow?

A. Yes; for it is not unusual for a shop to be occupied with the manufacture of one single shawl for a whole year, if it be a remarkably fine one.

Q. How can this be?

A. If elaborately worked, not one quarter of an inch is completed in one day by three persons: sometimes they are made in separate looms in different pieces, and afterwards beautifully joined together.

Q. Who may be said to have made shawls fashionable in Europe?

A. Josephine, the first wife of Napoleon Bonaparte, who brought her some exquisite specimens of them after his expedition to Egypt.

Q. To whose instruction was she indebted for the grace with which she wore them?

A. To General Rapp, who one evening

detained her a few moments from setting off to the opera to arrange one she had on in the manner of the Egyptian women.

Q. What destiny awaited upon the arrangement of this cashmere?

A. The life of Napoleon! the infernal machine exploded in vain! a moment sooner or later, and the shawl might have given another course to events, which would have changed the whole face of Europe.

Q. May not this event have created the passion for shawls Josephine afterwards testified?

A. Probably; for she left one hundred and fifty, all extremely beautiful, which after her death were sold much below their value.

Q. What ingenious invention gave great impetus to the cotton manufactures in England?

A. That of the carding engine, invented by James Hargreaves, about 1760, for straightening the cotton fibres; the same ingenious man invented the *Spinning Jenny*, by which a number of threads could be spun as easily as one.

Q. What cotton manufactures are the most famous in the world?

A. Those of Manchester and our manufacturing towns.

Q. How many spindles are daily at work in one of our large cotton mills?

A. About fifty thousand, and they will manufacture in a single day upwards of sixty thousand miles of cotton thread.

Q. Are not our commerce and national prosperity greatly promoted by the magnitude of our cotton manufactures?

A. Yes; for they are exported to the most distant parts of the world in exchange for the produce of other countries.

Q. What is silk?

A. The production of a caterpillar, called the silk-worm, which proceeds from the eggs of a moth.

Q. How are these little creatures managed?

A. Each moth lays about two hundred eggs: they are placed in houses in the midst of mulberry-trees, and are watched night and day.

Q. Is not the silk-worm a very curious insect?

A. Yes; from the little egg laid by the moth comes a small worm, which is fed with mulberry-leaves, chopped very fine, for about thirty days, when it is full grown, and becomes a large white worm.

Q. What does it do then?

A. It ceases to eat; it is then furnished with little brushes of heath or broom, on which it begins to form its silken ball.

Q. What next takes place?

A. On the third day it is hidden from sight, and on the tenth the work is finished.

Q. What are these balls now called?

A. Cocoons; and the worm in this state is called a chrysalis.

Q. What is done with the ball now?

A. The silk is wound off directly, or the worm would spoil it in trying to quit it.

Q. Pray is the worm killed?

A. No; it turns into a dark brown grub, which is again changed into a white moth.

Q. Does this curious insect undergo any other change?

A. No; the moth lays eggs for worms the next year, and then, in a very short time, dies.

Q. What places are noted for these insects?

A. China, the East Indies, the Levant, several parts of Italy, and the south of Spain.

Q. How was this valuable insect brought into Europe?

A. The eggs of the silk-worm were secretly and safely brought from China to Constantinople in the hollow of a cane, and soon multiplied abundantly.

Q. When did this happen?

A. In the reign of the Emperor Justinian, about A.D. 530.

Q. Is not the Morea celebrated for the culture of silk-worms?

A. Yes; the Morea was so named

from "Morea," the Greek for a mulberry-tree, great numbers of them growing there for the support of silk-worms.

Q. Pray to whom are the moderns indebted for the curious invention of the manufacture of silk from the produce of the silk-worm?

A. To the inhabitants of the Isle of Cos, in the Mediterranean Archipelago.

Q. From whence did they procure it?

A. From Serica, where the worm was a native; but it was long before the Romans would believe silk to be the work of a worm.

Q. Where was Serica?

A. It was a country of Asia, we are told, between the Ganges and the Eastern Ocean, generally thought to mean China.

Q. Was not silk very scarce for many ages?

A. Yes; it was sold for its weight in gold.

Q. What Roman emperor refused his empress a robe of purple silk on account of its enormous expense?

A. The Emperor Aurelian.

Q. Are not the first mulberry-trees ever planted in England still standing?

A. Yes; at Sion House, the seat of the Duke of Northumberland; the fruit has succeeded, but our climate is too cold and changeable to rear the silk-worm.

Q. Who introduced the silk-worm into France?

A. De Serres, but he met with much opposition even from the great Sully.

Q. But did not his master, Henry the Fourth, perceive the advantage it would prove to his country?

A. Yes; and he had mulberry-trees planted in all the royal gardens, and the eggs of silk-worms brought from Spain, by which means he added greatly to the national wealth of France, as silk is now one of her staple commodities.

Q. Who erected the first machine in England for the manufacturing of raw silk?

A. Sir Thomas Lombe, in 1719, at Derby, the model of which his brother

sent him from Italy, after working some
time there in one of their manufactories
in the meanest attire.

Q. What was its operation?

A. To wind, double, and twist the
silk, so as to render it fit for weaving;
before this discovery, we were obliged
to furnish our weavers with the material
from abroad.

Q. What risk did the high-spirited
youth expose himself to in attempting
this discovery?

A. Death; for the Italians had long
exclusively possessed the knowledge, and
enacted most severe laws to preserve it.

Q. How did young Lombe contrive
to become master of the secret?

A. He was engaged to superintend a
spinning engine, and after a time to
sleep in the mill; but of sleep he took
very little, for, providing himself with
matches and a dark lantern, he took
drawings of every important part of the
machinery, forwarded them to England,
and then made his escape.

Q. Did not this excite suspicion?

A. Yes; and it was thought of such importance that an Italian vessel was sent in pursuit; but he arrived safely in England.

Q. Did he live to see his mill in operation?

A. No; he was prematurely cut off by death, the effect, as was generally believed, of slow poison, administered by a person employed for the purpose by his enemies in Italy.

Q. When is the first record of silk being known in Britain?

A. As early as the year 780, Charlemagne sent Offa, king of Mercia, a present of a silken belt and two vests.

Q. What English king wore the first pair of knit silk stockings?

A. Henry II.; the invention of them came from Spain; but they were not heard of again till the reign of Henry VIII. and Edward VI.

Q. Who presented Edward VI. with a pair?

A. Sir Thomas Gresham, and they were much thought of.

Q. Who first wore tight silk stockings?

A. Catherine de Medicis: she was very vain of the symmetry of her hands and feet, and, amidst all her cares, her toilet took up much of her time and thoughts.

Q. Was not her dress very graceful?

A. Yes; and she was a great huntress, and introduced the use of the side-saddle.

Q. Who introduced the fashion of wearing black silk stockings into England?

A. Henrietta: her consort Charles I., and Charles II., seldom wore any other.

Q. What story is told of James I., whilst king of Scotland?

A. He borrowed of the Earl of Mar a pair of silk stockings, to receive the English ambassador, observing, "For ye would not, sure, that your king should appear as a scrub before strangers."

Q. How did he like them?

A. So well, that it is said he danced them into holes.

Q. What did Queen Elizabeth think of silk stockings?

A. In the third year of her reign she was furnished by her silk-woman with a pair, which she admired " as marvellous delicate wear," and she would never afterwards use cloth ones.

Q. Was not this queen very fond of dress?

A. Yes; it is said that after her death, three thousand different habits were found in her wardrobe.

Q. Were not some of her robes emblematical?

A. Yes; the lining of one of them was worked with eyes and ears, and on her arm a serpent was embroidered with pearls and rubies, holding a great ruby in its mouth.

Q. What were all these symbols to denote?

A. *Vigilance* and *Wisdom*.

Q. Who displeased this queen by preaching on the vanity of decking the body too finely?

A. One of her prelates. The queen

resented the hint, and told her ladies, "if the bishop held more discourse on such matters, she would fit him for heaven; but that he should walk thither without a staff, and leave his mantle behind him."

Q. Were not the ruffs of the ladies very large during Elizabeth's reign?

A. Yes; we are told that persons used to stand, by order of the queen, at the gates of the city, for the purpose of cutting down every ruff that was more than a yard in depth.

Q. How long did this ugly fashion last?

A. Only to the middle of the reign of James I., when a Mrs. Turner (an accomplice in poisoning Sir Thomas Overbury) being hanged in one, put them completely out of fashion.

Q. Is the use of the fan very ancient?

A. Yes; the custom was borrowed from the East, where the hot climate renders the use of fans and umbrellas indispensable to keep off the sun and flies.

Q. Of what materials are they made there ?

A. Principally of feathers; the most elegant are of peacocks'.

Q. Were not the fans very singular in the time of Queen Mary ?

A. Yes; the ladies carried fans with handles a yard long, and often used them to correct their children and servants.

Q. Are not fans indispensable to the dress of a Chinese ?

A. Yes; neither lady nor gentleman ever lays them aside, even in cold weather.

Q. What is poplin ?

A. A beautiful fabric woven from silk and worsted, or silk and wool, for which the Irish are greatly celebrated.

Q. What is velvet ?

A. A rich kind of stuff or silk, covered on the outside with a close, short, fine shag, the inside being a very short thick tissue.

Q. How is this shag or velveting made ?

A. It is formed of parts of the threads

of the warp, which the workman puts over a long narrow channelled ruler or needle, and afterwards cuts.

Q. How does he contrive to do this?

A. By drawing a sharp steel tool along the channel of the needle to the ends of the warp.

Q. Is not the work very tedious?

A. Yes; for during the process so many distinct operations are to be performed, that a very industrious weaver after a long day's work will have only woven a yard of plain velvet.

Q. Where are the principal and best manufactories of velvet?

A. In France and Italy, particularly at Venice, Milan, Florence, Genoa, and Lucca.

Q. What do you mean by a web?

A. It is a texture formed of threads, interwoven with each other: some of them are extended in length, and called the warp: and the others which are drawn across are called the woof or weft.

Q. How do they form patterns in weaving?

A. By throwing the woof, not over every other thread of the warp, but allowing two, three, or many more threads of the warp to remain unbound, by shooting the woof under them, and thus forming a pattern.

Q. What place is noted for the weaving of ribbons?

A. Coventry, in Warwickshire.

Q. What contributed to the full establishment of silk-weaving in this country?

A. The cruel treatment of the Protestant Christians in France, in 1685, on the revocation of the edict of Nantes.

Q. What was the edict of Nantes?

A. A law made by the good king Henry IV. of France, granting the Huguenots, or Protestants, the free use of their religion, and protecting their persons and property.

Q. What king was so foolish as to break this treaty?

A. Louis XIV. ; he treated the Protestants so ill, that they determined on leaving his kingdom.

Q. How many took refuge in England?

L

A. Upwards of 50,000 families, the chief part of whom had been silk-weavers.

Q. In which of our kings' reigns did this occur?

A. In James the Second's, though, being a rigid Catholic, it cannot be said that he encouraged them.

Q. Where are our largest silk manufactories?

A. At Manchester, and formerly Spitalfields in London was equally famous.

Q. What is brocade?

A. A costly stuff for dresses and furniture, formed of gold, silver, and silken threads, adorned with flowers and other figures: its expensiveness and liability to tarnish caused it to be discontinued.

Q. What is lace?

A. A work composed of many fine threads, interwoven by means of a number of bobbins, made of bone or ivory, each of which contains a small quantity of fine thread.

Q. How is the pattern of the lace formed?

A. The pattern is drawn upon a piece of stiff parchment pricked full of holes; and pins being stuck into these holes or openings, the threads are twisted round them, and the pattern formed.

Q. What parts of England are particularly famous for this manufacture?

A. The counties of Nottingham, Leicester, and Derby; Honiton in Devonshire is also celebrated for its lace; the county of Buckingham, once so famous for the manufacture, has almost ceased to produce lace.

Q. What foreign places have been long famous for rich costly lace?

A. Brussels, Antwerp, Valenciennes, and Mechlin, all places of note in Flanders.

Q. What is point lace?

A. It is seldom seen now; it is all worked stitch by stitch with the needle.

Q. Is there not an extensive manufactory of lace established at Limerick?

A. Yes, where point and Lisle lace are imitated with great accuracy; about twenty lace-workers were brought from Nottingham in 1829, and have proved eminently successful.

Q. What is tapestry?

A. A very curious kind of hangings, used many years ago to adorn and line the walls of a chamber.

Q. What is it composed of?

A. Wool and silk; frequently raised and enriched with gold and silver, representing figures of men, animals, landscapes, &c.

Q. Who are supposed to have been the first manufacturers of this beautiful and costly article?

A. The French and the Flemish, who are thought to have learnt the art in one of their crusades or expeditions against the Saracens.

Q. Did they not imitate by this work the paintings of the best masters?

A. Yes; and tapestry became one of the finest ornaments of palaces and churches.

Q. What great master has immortalized his name by his designs for tapestry?

A. Raphael, who executed 25 Scripture subjects as copies for tapestry hangings, at the request of Pope Leo X.; one set was intended to adorn the palace at Rome, the other as a present to Henry VIII. of England.

Q. Where were they sent to be woven?

A. To Arras, in the French province of Artois, some say to Brussels, at immense cost, being enriched with gold and silver.

Q. Are any of these splendid works still in existence?

A. Yes; they now adorn the galleries of the Vatican at Rome; during the sacking of that city by the French in 1798, they fell into the hands of an Italian Jew, who destroyed one for the sake of the gold and silver contained in the threads.

Q. Was not his avarice disappointed?

A. Yes; so he resold the rest at a high price to Pope Pius VII., who replaced them.

Q. Do we not possess some of these splendid designs?

A. Yes; the original 25 dwindled down to 10; and seven of them, denominated *Cartoons*, are preserved at Hampton Court; Rubens induced Charles I. to rescue them from oblivion, and to employ an experienced artist to repair them, as they had been pricked and mutilated by weavers in tracing the outline.

Q. What are cartoons?

A. Coloured designs drawn on strong paper or card-board, called by the French "carton;" they are most highly prized by all able to judge of their beauty, and are made before executing any great work in painting, fresco, or tapestry.

Q. Is there not a curious piece of tapestry preserved at Bayeux, in Normandy?

A. Yes; it is said to be the work of Matilda of Flanders, wife of William the Conqueror; it is upwards of 220 feet in length.

Q. What does it represent?

A. The conquest of England: the faces are supposed to be portraits.

Q. Who introduced tapestry into England?

A. Eleanor of Castile, the wife of Edward I. These early relics were not the production of the loom, but of the needle, for which the British ladies were particularly celebrated.

Q. Was there not a superb piece of tapestry in the late House of Lords?

A. Yes; it represented the defeat of the Spanish Armada, and was done for the Duke of Nottingham, then High Admiral of England, at a cost of 2000*l*., and afterwards sold by him to King James I.

Q. Is the manufacture of tapestry still encouraged?

A. No; the Gobelins manufactory in Paris is the only one now in Europe; it is carried there to such perfection, that the colouring and beauty of the pieces are equal to the fine paintings from which they are copied.

Q. When was the Gobelin tapestry introduced into France?

A. In the reign of Francis I., by Giles

Gobelin, a celebrated dyer, particularly in worsteds, who brought to the greatest perfection the fine scarlet dye, which still bears his name.

Q. How was this dye discovered?

A. Gobelin procured it from a man at Leghorn, whose father discovered it by chance.

Q. By what means?

A. He had a phial of aqua-regia standing in a window framed with tin, in which was some extract of cochineal; a piece of the tin being loose, fell into the phial of aqua-regia, and changed its colour to a beautiful brilliant scarlet.

Q. Was the tin imagined to have this extraordinary effect upon the cochineal?

A. Yes; and by many experiments it was found to be the chief agent in this chemical change.

Q. Where may be seen now a splendid display of Gobelin tapestry?

A. At Windsor Castle; some of it was a present from Charles X. of France to the late Queen Adelaide.

Q. Can articles from the Gobelin tapestry be purchased?

A. No; the French government support this national manufactory, and most of the pieces when completed are designed for presents to distinguished courts; their value is enormous, as one piece occupies from two to six years, according to its size.

Q. Does one workman accomplish a whole design?

A. No; several are employed, one doing the eye, another the mouth, another the hands, &c.; then there are a set of workmen called *fine-drawers*, who unite the pieces with such nicety that no join is perceptible.

Q. What is wool?

A. The curled hair or covering of sheep.

Q. How is it prepared?

A. It is first sorted, then scoured and washed, afterwards dried in the shade, well beaten, and the dirt picked out.

Q. What is next done?

A. It is oiled, combed, and spun

on a wheel; then sized or stiffened a little, when it is fit for weaving into cloth.

Q. Is the cloth then fit for use?

A. No; after it is woven, it is washed with soap and water several times, and dried after each washing.

Q. Is it not fit then to make into cloth for coats?

A. No; it must still be dyed, brushed, and pressed.

Q. Whence have we the best wool?

A. From Spain and from Australia; but England has long been famous for wool.

Q. What English sovereigns gave great encouragement to the woollen manufacture?

A. Edward III. and Queen Elizabeth. They received the poor people from the Netherlands, and allowed them to establish large manufactories at Norwich, and other places.

Q. What is Merino wool?

A. The wool of a famous Spanish breed of sheep, of which the very finest cloths are made.

Q. What are the principal articles in which wool is used?

A. Woollen cloth of all kinds, flannels, blankets, kerseymeres, worsted stockings, druggets, baize, merinos, besides many shawls, handkerchiefs, dresses, &c.

Q. What is teasel?

A. A very valuable plant, without which our woollen manufactory could hardly have made any progress.

Q. Why is it so valuable?

A. Because the crooked scales connected with the flowers are so hard and rough that the heads are employed for raising the nap on woollen cloths.

Q. How are they used?

A. Many of these heads are fixed in a frame, and with this the surface of the cloth is *teased* or brushed until all the ends of the wool are drawn out, and the loose parts' combed off, and the cloth ceases to yield impediments to the free passage of the wheel, or frame of teasels.

Q. Have not hitherto all mechanical

inventions failed to effect the same purpose as this natural production ?

A. Yes; all the machines that have been tried offer too great resistance to the knots, and instead of yielding and breaking as the teasel does, tear them out, making a hole and injuring the surface.

Q. Does not the dressing of a piece of cloth consume a great number of teasels?

A. Yes; from fifteen hundred to two thousand heads.

Q. Where are teasels cultivated ?

A. In some of the strong clay lands of Wiltshire, Essex, Gloucester, and Somerset ; they require constant labour through most part of the year, and hence loss, or great profit, depends upon circumstances.

Q. If our own crop fail, from whence do we procure teasels ?

A. From Holland and France.

Q. Where were blankets first made ?

A. At Bristol; they are so named from Thomas Blanket, who, in 1340, first set up the looms there for weaving these comfortable articles.

Q. Where are the finest blankets now made?

A. At Witney, in Oxfordshire.

Q. What is worsted?

A. Twisted wool: it has its name from a village in Norfolk, near Norwich, where it was first invented; when intended for embroidery, it is dyed after it is spun.

Q. What is bunting?

A. A thin but very tough woollen stuff, used for the various sorts of flags.

Q. Are not Scottish plaids made of wool?

A. Yes.

Q. What is leather?

A. It is made of the skin of different animals.

Q. How is it prepared?

A. First, the hair is taken off, by steeping it in lime water, and then scraping it clean with a knife.

Q. What else must be done?

A. It is laid open in a pit, then covered with tan or oak-bark and the pit filled with water, where it remains from one to three or four years.

Q. Has not this process been recently much shortened?

A. Yes; by the use of a concentrated solution of bark instead of bark steeped in water.

Q. Is it now finished?

A. No; it is greased, waxed, blacked, and dyed.

Q. What is Morocco leather?

A. The skin of goats, dressed, tanned, and dyed in a peculiar manner, invented in Morocco, whence it has its name.

Q. Is not this leather beautifully made in London?

A. Yes.

Q. Why are goat-skins used?

A. Because they take the dye better, and produce richer and more brilliant colours.

Q. Where is Morocco?

A. A large country in Barbary.

Q. Does not the country called Barbary include several kingdoms?

A. Yes; the northern coast of Africa,

extending along the sea-shore of the Mediterranean, is so called: it is nearly two thousand miles in length.

Q. By what names are the several kingdoms known?

A. Barca, Tripoli, Tunis, Algiers, and Morocco.

Q. How did the ancients call this country of Barbary?

A. By the names of Mauritania, Numidia, and Libya.

Q. Has not the coast of Barbary been infested with pirates in modern times?

A. Yes; and the Dey of Algiers reduced all his Christian prisoners into slavery.

Q. Did not our Government interfere?

A. Yes; and upon August 27th, 1816, the British fleet, under Lord Exmouth, bombarded and entirely destroyed the fortifications of Algiers and the fleet of the Dey, and compelled him to liberate all Christian captives.

Q. Did the Dey keep his promise to desist from piracy?

A. No; and Algeria has now therefore been converted into a French province.

Q. What is chamois leather?

A. A warm, pliable leather, dressed in oil, or tanned, and much valued for its softness and being capable of bearing soap.

Q. What sort of animal is the chamois?

A. A kind of antelope, about the size of a goat; these animals inhabit mountainous places, particularly the Alps and Pyrenees.

Q. Is it not a dangerous pursuit to hunt them?

A. Yes; for they go in large companies, and take fright at the least noise, and can spring at a single leap up rocks more than twenty feet high.

Q. But is not chamois leather now made from the skins of other animals?

A. Yes; from those of deer, sheep, and goats; a common description of this leather is often called wash-leather.

Q. What is tanning?

A. The art of converting the raw skins of animals into leather.

Q. What is buck-skin and doe-skin?

A. The hide of the deer; it is manufactured into breeches and gloves, on account of its softness.

Q. What is the doe?

A. The female deer; its young one is called a fawn.

Q. What is a hat?

A. A covering for the head, made of wool and hair mixed curiously together by means of beating, pressing, boiling, and soaking.

Q. Of the hair of what animal are men's hats made?

A. The finest and most valued are made of the pure hair of an animal called the castor or beaver.

Q. What sort of an animal is this?

A. An amphibious one, remarkable for its art, address, and contrivance in building its habitation.

Q. What country is it a native of?

A. Canada, and other provinces of North America.

Q. What do you mean by amphibious?

A. Being able to live both upon land and in the water, like frogs, tortoises, otters, &c.

Q. What other animals afford hair fit for making hats?

A. The rabbit, hare, and goat; their fur or skin on this account is very valuable.

Q. Is not the hair of these animals mixed with much wool?

A. Yes; they are entangled together, pressed and beaten into a sort of cloth of which the hat is made.

Q. What is this cloth called?

A. Felt; a little of the real beaver hair is added to the outside to make it very soft and glossy.

Q. Has not the use of beaver hats been to a considerable extent superseded?

A. Yes; by silk hats, the exterior of which is covered with a nap made of silk plush.

Q. How are the hats made of such a beautiful black?

A. By dyeing, which is done by boiling them in logwood, and afterwards dipping them into a preparation of copperas, commonly called blue vitriol.

Q. What is logwood?

A. The wood of a low prickly tree, of a deep red colour, found in great plenty at Campeachy, and in the bay of Honduras.

Q. Is it not in high request among dyers?

A. Yes; especially in dyeing black; but it is used in making purple, violet, and many other fine colours.

Q. What did men and women wear before hats were invented?

A. Hoods of various colours, and close-knit woollen caps.

Q. Who is said to have introduced the fashion of wearing hats?

A. Charles VII. of France; he made his public entry into Rouen, in 1449, wearing a hat lined with red velvet and ornamented with a plume of feathers.

Q. May the use of hats and caps be dated from this time?

A. Certainly; for they soon became

general. Charles VII. of France lived
in the reign of our Henry VI.

Q. What are gloves?

A. A covering for the hands and arms.

Q. From the skins of what animals
are leather gloves made?

A. From the kid, lamb, doe, and elk.

Q. What is a kid?

A. A young goat.

Q. What is a lamb?

A. A young sheep.

Q. What is a doe?

A. The female of a rabbit, as well as
of a deer, is called a doe; but it is of the
skin of the latter that gloves are made.

Q. What is an elk?

A. A large kind of deer, the size of a
horse; it inhabits the northern latitudes
of Europe, America, and Asia, and feeds
on twigs and branches of trees.

Q. Is it a gentle creature?

A. Yes, except when teased by the
gadfly; it travels at the rate of fifty
miles a day, in a kind of shambling trot.

Q. Where are gloves principally
made?

A. At Worcester, Hereford, Hexham, and Woodstock; Limerick, in Ireland, was famous for them for above a century.

Q. Can that article now be procured there?

A. With difficulty: for the manufactory of them is removed to Cork: the leather and workmanship of these noted gloves is so fine and delicate, that a pair may be passed through a wedding-ring or enclosed in a walnut-shell.

Q. Where is Hexham?

A. In Northumberland, formerly celebrated for the forest where Queen Margaret met the robber.

Q. Where is Woodstock?

A. In Oxfordshire; the celebrated Fair Rosamond lived there in the time of Henry II.

Q. Were not the gloves of nobles highly ornamented in our early reigns?

A. Yes; they were richly embroidered with gold, and those appropriated to royalty had jewels on the back of the hand.

Q. Is it not recorded that Cœur de Lion owed his captivity to the fatal carelessness of his page, who sought the market-place with his master's gloves hanging to his girdle ?

A. Yes ; the jewelled glove betrayed the royal station of the pilgrim, and the Duke of Austria exclaimed, "*It is none other than Richard.*"

Q. Who presented a beautiful pair of perfumed and embroidered gloves to Queen Elizabeth ?

A. Edward, Earl of Oxford ; she was so pleased with them, that she sat for her portrait with them on her hands.

Q. What act of gallantry is recorded in the history of needlework respecting one of her gloves ?

A. That as the Earl of Cumberland stood before Elizabeth, she dropped her glove, and on his picking it up, graciously desired him to keep it. He caused the trophy to be encircled with diamonds, and ever after, at all tilts and tourneys, bore it conspicuously placed in front of his high-crowned hat.

Q. What is meant by the gauntlet?

A. It was a glove of jointed steel plates, which was worn of old by knights in armour.

Q. What use did they occasionally make of it?

A. To throw it down to any one who had offended them, as a sign that they were to fight till one was slain, or confessed himself vanquished.

Q. Were not gloves in use in very early times?

A. Yes; Xenophon tells us that the Persians used gloves, and cites it as a proof of their effeminacy; and Cicero tells us of their long-standing use among the Romans.

Q. When did gloves first form a necessary part of female dress?

A. Not until the reign of Queen Anne; they were then richly worked and embroidered, and were so expensive that they were a customary new year's gift.

Q. What are stockings?

A. Coverings for the feet and legs.

M 6

Q. Of what were they first made?

A. Of cloth, or of stuffs sewed together.

Q. Who invented the art of weaving stockings in a frame?

A. William Lee, a native of Woodborough, near Nottingham, in 1589, in the reign of Queen Elizabeth.

Q. Was he not very ill-treated for his ingenious invention?

A. Yes; the stocking-knitters fearing it would spoil their trade, drove him away.

Q. What became of him?

A. He died of grief, but his invention did not die with him.

Q. What places are noted for our manufacture of cotton stockings?

A. Nottingham, and Aberdeen in Scotland.

Q. Of what different materials have shoes been made?

A. Of raw skins, rushes, broom, paper, flax, silk, wood, iron, silver, and gold; they are now usually made of leather, stuff, and silk.

Q. Have not their shape, colour, and ornaments been very various?

A. Yes; they have been square, high, low, long, cut, and curved.

Q. What distinguishing ornament did the Patricians, among the Romans, wear in their shoes?

A. An ivory crescent: and Isaiah speaks of the moons which the Jewish women wore in their shoes.

Q. What did the Egyptians use for shoes?

A. The bark of the papyrus, a rush growing on the banks of the river Nile.

Q. What is the custom of the Turks when they enter their mosques?

A. They always put off their shoes, and leave them at the door.

Q. How were shoes adorned in England in the reign of Edward IV.?

A. With long peaks turning upwards from the toe, and fastened by silver chains or laces to the knees.

Q. Did not a contrary extreme become the fashion?

A. Yes; and in a few years all the fine gentlemen looked as if they had got the gout; for they wore cloth and velvet shoes so very broad, that their feet looked like great platters.

Q. Was not a law now obliged to be made?

A. Yes; forbidding any shoe to be more than six inches across the toes.

Q. Were not the shoes and boots highly ornamented in the reign of Queen Elizabeth?

A. Yes; the boots at this time had immense tops turned down and fringed, made of cloth or leather, embroidered in gold and silver and various coloured silks. They would cost from four to ten pounds a pair.

Q. Of what is the upper leather of men's shoes usually made?

A. Of calf-skin: ladies' shoes are made of kid, morocco, jean, satin, and velvet.

Q. Was not dress in the reigns of Edward IV. and his brother Richard III. very ridiculous?

A. Yes; it was so tight, that persons resembled stuffed figures more than living men ; their shoulders were stuffed out to make them look broad, and the waist was pinched in as tight as it could be borne.

Q. Were not the sleeves to this dress enormously long ?

A. Yes ; they were worn hanging from the elbow such a length, that Edward IV. used to tie his behind his back, to avoid tumbling over them.

Q. Are not the beef-eaters, as they are called, still in the dress of the time of Henry VIII. ?

A. Yes ; the style of dress was then very showy, and because the king was so fat, the courtiers stuffed out their clothes to make themselves look as big as he did.

Q. Were not the sleeves to this dress ridiculously tight ?

A. Yes ; it is said that some of the beaux had them sewed up every time they put them on.

Q. Was not Henry VIII. a tyrant even in taste ?

A. Yes ; he made arbitrary laws to regulate the dress of his subjects.

Q. How ?

A. Cloth of gold or tissue was reserved for dukes and marquises ; if of a purple colour, for the royal family. Silks and velvets were only to be worn by commoners of distinction, and embroidery was forbidden to all beneath an earl.

Q. From what arose the name of beef-eater ?

A. It is a very strange corruption of a very plain word, " buffetier," a person who waits at a buffet, or sideboard, as our butlers do now.

Q. Where are these entertaining accounts to be met with ?

A. In Mrs. Markham's clever history of England.

Q. What are pins made of?

A. Brass drawn out into wire, which, when the pin is finished, is whitened.

Q. Does not a pin, before it is fit for use, pass through the hands of many workmen ?

A. Yes; a great many workmen are employed upon each pin, between the drawing of the brass wire, and the sticking of the pin in the paper.

Q. How does this happen?

A. When the wire is drawn fine enough, it must be made straight; then cut into proper lengths, afterwards sharpened at the points, then the head is put on; and, lastly, it is whitened and polished.

Q. When were pins first used and made?

A. They were invented in France, in 1543, in the reign of Francis I.; before this art was discovered the ladies used small skewers made of wood, bone, and ivory.

Q. What queen first made use of pins in England?

A. Catherine Howard, the fifth wife of Henry VIII.

Q. Were they not considered a great luxury, and not fit for common use?

A. Yes; the maker was not allowed to sell them in an open shop, except on two days of the year, at the beginning of January.

Q. What old custom did this give rise to?

A. To husbands giving their wives money at the beginning of the year, to buy a few pins; therefore money allowed to a wife for her own private spending is even now called *pin-money*.

Q. Where is there a great manufacture of pins?

A. At Gloucester.

Q. What are needles?

A. A needle is a small instrument made of steel, pointed at one end, and pierced at the other for the thread.

Q. What steel makes the best needles?

A. The German and Hungarian steel.

Q. When were needles first made in England?

A. In the reign of Queen Mary, by a negro from Spain; but as he would never tell the secret, it was lost at his death.

Q. When was this useful art recovered?

A. In the reign of Queen Elizabeth, when Elias Growse, a German, taught the art to the English, who have since brought it to perfection; before the sixteenth century not a needle was to be had but of foreign manufacture, and then a needle was looked upon as "*a domestic treasure.*"

Q. What sort of needles did people use before the invention of steel ones?

A. Those made of thorns, fish-bones, &c.—rudely sharpened at one end. Captain Cook found the inhabitants of the Sandwich Islands using such when he first visited them.

Q. Are not many thousand men, women, and children, employed in making needles?

A. Yes; this useful little article

passes through many hands, and requires the greatest nicety in making.

Q. Where are needles chiefly
made?

A. At Redditch, in the county of
Worcester, and other neighbouring
places.

Q. Which is the easiest to make, a
pin or a needle?

A. A pin; and a machine has
been lately invented, which performs
a considerable portion of the operation of pin-making without manual
labour.

Q. Who invented thimbles?

A. The Dutch: they were introduced
into England by John Lofling, a me-
chanic from Holland, who commenced
business at Islington, about the year
1695.

Q. Is not the quantity of wire used
in our different manufactories enormous?

A. Yes; besides the strings of musical instruments, pins and needles, and
countless other small wares, the cotton

manufacture consumes a very large quantity.

Q. What is catgut?

A. This is a name given to small strings for violins and other instruments, formerly made from the skins of the intestines of cats.

Q. But what is now chiefly used?

A. The intestines of sheep or lambs, dried and twisted, either singly, or several together.

Q. What places are famous for making it?

A. Lyons in France; Italy, and Germany.

Q. Who invented musical notes?

A. Guido Aretine, an Italian monk, in the reign of Henry I.; he formed the musical scale we now use, an invention which he thought "atoned for all his sins."

Q. What is whalebone?

A. A sort of gristle found inside the whale in thin, long, flat pieces, three or four yards long : it supplies the place of teeth.

Q. Are there not four hundred or five hundred of them in one whale?

A. Yes; they stick to the upper jaw, and form a kind of strainer to keep in the sea-snails and other small creatures upon which whales live.

Q. What is whalebone used for?

A. To stiffen stays, umbrellas, and whips.

Q. Are not umbrellas of great antiquity?

A. Yes; the Greeks, Romans, and all eastern nations used them to keep off the sun; "ombrello," in Italian, signifies " *a little shade.*"

Q. Did not the use of this article travel from Italy into the other countries of Europe?

A. Yes; but very slowly, for they have scarcely been used in England above eighty years.

Q. Is whalebone used in the manufacture of whip handles?

A. Yes; the handles of riding whips and waggoners' whips are made of several slips of whalebone, each smaller towards the point, bound together by a sort of network woven round them.

Q. What is the lash made of?

A. A piece of whip-cord; and its length and quality depend upon the purpose it is to be used for.

Q. What place is famous for whips?

A. Daventry, in Northamptonshire.

Q. What is a cable?

A. A strong thick rope made of hemp, or an iron chain, fastened to a ship's anchor.

Q. What are its uses?

A. To hold ships firm at anchor, and to tow vessels in large rivers. Every great ship has cables of various sizes.

Q. At what place in England are they principally manufactured?

A. At Deptford, in Kent.

Q. Of what are the strongest cables now made?

A. Of iron wire.

Q. What is a telescope?

A. It is an optical instrument of

many glasses, which brings objects at a great distance close to our view.

Q. Who invented it?

A. Zachariah Jansen, a Hollander of Middleburgh, in Zealand, and by trade a spectacle-maker. But Roger Bacon knew of the principle of the telescope.

Q. How did Jansen discover it?

A. Without any premeditated design: for having placed two spectacle glasses at a certain distance opposite each other, he perceived that the two glasses in that situation magnified objects considerably.

Q. How did he proceed?

A. He fixed glasses in that manner, and in the year 1590 made a telescope of the length of twelve inches; such was its origin.

Q. Who greatly improved it?

A. Galileo, who was the first that brought it to any degree of perfection.

Q. Who was he?

A. An Italian educated at Florence.

Q. Did he suffer much from great

study, and the constant use of his glasses ?

A. Yes ; he became quite blind.

Q. Who has since brought the telescope to very great perfection ?

A. Doctor Herschel ; but great improvements have been made since his time, particularly by Lord Rosse.

Q. Did not the invention of the telescope lead to that of the microscope ?

A. Yes ; Jansen, the ingenious inventor, did in little what had been done in large, and from thence came the microscope.

Q. What is a microscope?

A. An instrument which magnifies the smallest objects, so as to render them clear to the sight.

Q. Are we not greatly indebted to these two instruments for much valuable knowledge ?

A. Yes ; to the telescope for the wonderful knowledge we have gained of the heavens, and to the microscope for that of a new little world.

N

Q. Are we to believe that we see every thing that inhabits the earth?

A. No; we see many species of animals, from the elephant to the mite, and there our sight ends:—but at the mite begins an infinite multitude of animals which our eyes cannot discern without the aid of the microscope.

Q. What is the kaleidoscope?

A. A beautiful instrument composed of mirrors and reflectors placed in a tube, at the end of which are small pieces of coloured glass.

Q. By whom was it invented?

A. By Sir David Brewster, about the year 1815.

Q. Is it not very useful as well as amusing?

A. Yes; for the beautiful objects it produces in endless variety often suggest patterns which are adopted in our arts and manufactures.

Q. What is the barometer?

A. An instrument for telling the changes in the weather, by means of the variations in the state of the air.

Q. Who invented it?

A. Torricelli, the pupil of Galileo, in the year 1644.

Q. What does the name signify?

A. A *measure of weight;* it is compounded of two Greek words.

Q. What is the thermometer?

A. An instrument for measuring the degree of heat or cold, by the rising or falling of the mercury.

Q. What is a clock?

A. A machine for measuring time, regulated by the uniform motion of a pendulum.

Q. What is a pendulum?

A. A heavy weight which swings backwards and forwards, so that one tooth of the wheel, which makes a tick, escapes every time that the pendulum beats.

Q. What is the difference between a clock and a watch?

A. A watch cannot have a pendulum, because it would not go unless kept upright: it is therefore moved by a spring instead of a weight.

Q. How then is its motion governed?

A. By a balance instead of a pendulum : the balance is a small wheel.

Q. When were clocks first manufactured in England?

A. About 1368, when Edward III. allowed three artists from Delft, in Holland, to practise their occupation in this country.

Q. Where were the first two clocks placed that were known in England?

A. One over the gateway at Westminster, and the other at Canterbury, in the time of Henry III.

Q. When were pocket watches first brought into England?

A. About the year 1577, in the reign of Elizabeth : they were invented at Nuremberg, in Franconia, in Germany.

Q. What great emperor amused himself by making watches ?

A. Charles the Fifth of Germany : he one day exclaimed, " What an egregious fool must I have been, to have squandered so much blood and treasure in an absurd attempt to make all men think alike, when I cannot even make a few watches keep time together!"

Q. What is china-ware, or porcelain, made of?

A. A hard rocky stone of the nature of flint, ground to a fine powder, mixed with a sort of clay which is quite soft.

Q. Does not the beauty of the china depend upon the mixing of these materials?

A. Yes; for making the finer sort they put half and half of each.

Q. How is it made into the many shapes we see it in?

A. It is mixed into a fine paste, well kneaded with the hands, after which it is moulded into shapes, then painted, gilded, and, lastly, baked in a furnace.

Q. But is it not partially baked before it is painted, &c.?

A. Yes; in which state it is called biscuit.

Q. What do they use in England for the making of china?

A. A kind of clay and ground flint.

Q. Why is it called china-ware?

A. Because the first brought into Europe came from China; and the Chinese still excel in this manufacture.

Q. Is not England famous for its blue and white ware, so cheap and common in every house?

A. Yes; it is made thus: the pattern intended for the plate, &c., is first engraved on a copper plate, which is then spread over with some thick blue colouring: upon this a very thin paper well soaped is placed, and passed under a rolling press, leaving the wet impression of the pattern on the paper.

Q. What then?

A. This paper is immediately transferred to the plate in a state of *biscuit*, which being porous receives the tint and pattern, and after being baked and glazed, looks as if it had been painted with a brush: a variety of colours may be used, but blue is the most common.

Q. What is the word porcelain supposed to be derived from?

A. The Portuguese word *porceluna*, which means a *cup*, because the Portuguese were the first who traded to China, and the chief articles they brought over were cups.

Q. What is the distinction between earthenware and porcelain?

A. Porcelain is a half-vitrified substance, in a middle state between *thick* earthenware and *clear* glass, and produces a semi-transparent material.

Q. Why is the ugly dragon china from China so much valued?

A. Because it is so difficult to procure, the hideous figure on it being the imperial arms, and only permitted for the emperor's use.

Q. Has England any occasion now to go abroad for this beautiful ware?

A. No; our own manufactures at Derby and Worcester surpass most others in taste, elegance, and beauty.

Q. Where are our earthenware, porcelain, and pottery chiefly manufactured?

A. In a district in Staffordshire, called the Potteries; which supplies not only England, but also foreign countries with large quantities of these useful manufactures.

Q. Is there not a beautiful ware made in France?

A. Yes; it is called Sèvres china, and is very expensive, as well as that made at Dresden, in Saxony.

Q. What peculiarity distinguishes the Dresden china?

A. The raised figures and flowers on its surface, coloured so delicately and true to nature, that the ornamental specimens are most beautiful.

Q. Is not the Sèvres manufactory near Paris carried on at the public expense?

A. Yes; and no cost is spared to carry it to perfection; but the exorbitant price of the smallest article places it beyond the reach of general visitors; a single plate sells for 20*l*., and vases, &c., from 100*l*. to 1000*l*.; like the Gobelin tapestry, they are often sent as royal gifts.

Q. What great man in England possessed magnificent services in Dresden and Sèvres?

A. The late Duke of Wellington, presented to him by the King of Prussia and the King of France.

Q. What is Delf or Dutch ware?

A. Baked clay or pottery, covered with a thick white or brown glazing within and without. It is an ancient European production, invented in 1450, and was formerly carried to great perfection in Holland.

Q. Are Dutch tiles made of this material?

A. Yes; they formerly ornamented fire-places, and are still used to line dairies and baths.

Q. What ancient nations have been celebrated for their pottery?

A. The Egyptians, from whom the Greeks learnt it, whence it passed into Etruria, now called Tuscany, whose vessels have served for models to the present day for the elegance of their shape; many are to be seen in the British Museum.

Q. Is there not a famous pagoda at Nankin, which is covered with a coating of china?

A. Yes; it is two hundred feet high, and consists of nine stories; it has been built upwards of 400 years, and is held sacred by the Chinese.

Q. Does it not retain all the freshness of a newly-erected building?

A. Yes; it is also sometimes illuminated, as it contains 142 lamps fixed in niches, burning nine gallons of oil for a single night's consumption.

Q. What is glass?

A. A mixture made by melting flint, sand, and alkali in a very hot furnace.

Q. What is alkali or kali?

A: A kind of salt, found in the ashes of burnt vegetables.

Q. What alkalies are chiefly used in glass and soap manufactories?

A. Potash and soda.

Q. How did man become acquainted with the beautiful discovery of glass?

A. Accident made it known to some merchants in Syria, who were ship-wrecked on that shore.

Q. How?

A. Finding plenty of the plant kali,

they used it for making a fire on the ground, and the ashes mixing with the sand produced this beautiful substance.

Q. Was the first glass that was made transparent?

A. No; it was more like what we call enamel, being perfectly opaque, and varying much in colour.

Q. Have not some very ancient specimens been discovered?

A. Yes; in the Egyptian tombs, and other buildings of remote antiquity.

Q. Are not some of these to be seen in England?

A. Yes; in the British Museum.

Q. When was the art of making it transparent discovered?

A. Not till several centuries afterwards, and who the discoverer was is unknown.

Q. What sum of money did the Emperor Nero give for two small cups of transparent glass?

A. It is recorded in history that he paid a sum of money for them nearly equal to 50,000*l*. sterling.

Q. How is glass made into so many curious forms?

A. By blowing, and when made hot can be cut with a pair of scissors or shears.

Q. Are not all these curious shapes baked?

A. Yes; or they would fall to pieces.

Q. When were drinking-glasses first made in England?

A. In Queen Mary's time; but glass drinking-cups were in use from the time of the Saxons.

Q. Were looking-glasses common in the reign of Queen Mary?

A. No; there were a few used at the toilet, but they were very small; the ladies usually carried them in their pockets, or hung them to their girdles.

Q. When were glass windows used in England?

A. About the time of William Rufus, and they were considered as a mark of great magnificence, suitable only to palaces and churches.

Q. Where were the first glass windows put that were ever seen in England?

A. At Hexham Abbey in Northumberland; they were made by some workmen who came from France, and who taught the English; but it was long before they became common.

Q. What nation first used this beautiful substance for windows?

A. The Italians: in a short time the French learned to make it, and from them the art travelled to England.

Q. Were not glass windows in dwelling-houses considered moveable furniture?

A. Yes; for when the Earl of Northumberland, in the reign of Queen Elizabeth in 1573, left Alnwick Castle, the windows were taken out of their frames and laid carefully by.

Q. When were such windows introduced into common houses?

A. Not till the early part of the reign of Charles I.; and were not general till the end of Queen Anne's reign.

Q. When was plate-glass first cast in England?

A. In the reign of Charles II., by some Venetian artists, brought to London by the Duke of Buckingham.

Q. Do we not now excel foreigners in the manufacture of glass?

A. Yes; but in all that relates to the colouring or staining of glass, the Bohemians are at present our superiors.

Q. What city was long famed for the fineness of its looking-glasses?

A. Venice.

Q. Where is Venice?

A. In Italy; a rich and celebrated city, built on seventy-two little islands.

Q. Were not horn and oiled paper used as substitutes for glass in windows?

A. Yes; the horn was heated till quite a jelly, when it became thin and transparent, sufficient to keep out cold and admit light; at present it is used for common lanterns.

Q. What is horn?

A. A substance growing on the heads

of various animals, serving them as weapons, both of offence and defence.

Q. Are horns of any great use?

A. Yes; for when strongly heated, or soaked in boiling water, they become very soft, and may be pressed into moulds of various forms, such as handles for knives, forks, &c.

Q. Have not horns been used for various purposes?

A. Yes; there are drinking horns, hunting horns, and in olden times horns were used for summoning the people.

Q. Is not the use of drinking horns very ancient?

A. Yes; they were in very common use amongst our Saxon ancestors, who frequently had them gilded, and magnificently ornamented; they often had a screw at the end, which being taken off, they were converted into hunting horns.

Q. What is kelp?

A. Burnt sea-weed, which contains carbonate of soda: the making of kelp once afforded employment to many industrious families in Scotland and the Orkneys.

Q. What are the Orkney Islands?

A. A cluster of small islands to the north of Scotland.

Q. What is horse-hair?

A. The hair of the mane and tail of the horse.

Q. What is it useful for?

A. That of the mane is used for stuffing mattresses, chair bottoms, saddles, and horse-collars.

Q. And what is the hair in the tail used for?

A. It is woven into a kind of cloth for covering chairs and sofas, and for making fishing lines, sieves, and the bows of musical instruments.

Q. What is a carpet?

A. A covering for the floor, either worked with a needle, or woven in a loom.

Q. What is the meaning of the word carpet?

A. It is derived from an old Italian word " *carpetta*," " *car-pita* " signifying a covering for floors.

Q. What eastern countries have been noted for their carpets?

A. Persia and Turkey; some of the former are exquisitely beautiful.

Q. Are not Turkey carpets of peculiar texture?

A. Yes; they are made entirely of wool, and are much thicker, warmer, and stronger than any other; they are principally made near Smyrna.

Q. How are the beautiful patterns formed?

A. The workman has a painting traced in its proper colours tied before him, which is divided into little squares, by which he knows how many stitches he is to use of one colour.

Q. How is Brussels carpet manufactured?

A. Brussels carpeting is made by passing the threads over a wire, which is afterwards drawn out, leaving a row of loops.

Q. Where are Brussels carpets chiefly manufactured?

A. At Kidderminster in Worcestershire.

Q. What are the Wilton or Pile carpets?

A. They are made like the Brussels carpeting, only the loops are cut before the wires are drawn out.

Q. Are they not very handsome?

A. Yes; they look like rich velvet.

Q. What is peculiar in the Axminster carpets?

A. They are woven without a seam to any pattern, and are exceedingly beautiful and expensive.

Q. Is not England celebrated for her carpets?

A. Yes; but it is not in beauty, design, or execution, that we excel our continental neighbours, who are most ingenious in this manufacture, but they want our fine material; for it is the cheapness and beauty of our wool which enable us to make them in great variety, and much more reasonable.

Q. Were carpets used by the ancients?

A. Yes; they are mentioned in the Bible, as used by persons who dwelt in tents; and the Romans among their luxuries reckoned the Babylonian carpets; even at this day the towns bordering on the ruins of Babylon and Nineveh excel in the beauty of their carpets.

Q. But when were they first used in England?

A. It is uncertain; so late as the twelfth century it was considered a great luxury to have the floors covered even with clean straw.

Q. Is not this mentioned as an instance of the haughty Becket's splendid style of living?

A. Yes; his sumptuous apartments were every day in winter strewed with clean straw or hay, and in summer with green rushes.

Q. Why?

A. That the gentlemen who paid court to him, and who could not find a place at his table, might not soil their fine clothes by sitting on a dirty floor.

Q. What places in England were formerly famous for carpets?

A. Axminster, Wilton, and Kidderminster: the two latter places are still so: the art was brought to London in 1750, in the reign of George II., by two men from France.

Q. Where are carpets now chiefly manufactured in Great Britain?

A. At Glasgow and Kilmarnock in Scotland, and at Wilton, Cirencester, and Worcester; but Brussels carpets are mostly manufactured at Kidderminster.

Q. What is dyeing?

A. The art of staining silk, cloth, or linen of various colours, by the mixture of different materials.

Q. How many colours are there that cannot be made by any mixture?

A. Three: red, blue, and yellow: but they serve, mixed with a variety of other things, to form every other shade in colours.

Q. What will blue and yellow make?

A. Green; and if blue and red are mixed they will produce purple; and red and yellow will form orange.

Q. Is the art of dyeing of very great antiquity?

A. Yes; it was practised in the earliest ages by the Jews, and by the Babylonians and the Egyptians.

Q. Was it not equally well known in Hindostan, Ceylon, and China?

A. Yes; and carried by them to the greatest perfection; and when Mexico was discovered, the art of dyeing or painting was equally well known to the inhabitants.

Q. How was this proved?

A. By their sending information of the arrival of the Spanish squadron on their coast to Montezuma, by means of painting exact representations of their ships on cloth.

Q. Did they not by means of this kind of picture-writing keep their records, histories, and calendars?

A. Yes; they represented things that had bodily shapes in their proper figures and colours; and those that had none by some characters well understood.

o 5

Q. What country was celebrated for the richness of its purple dye, so much valued by the ancients?

A. Egypt; it was obtained from a shell-fish, called murex, or the purple fish.

Q. Are there many different species of this fish?

A. Yes; and it is thought by this they obtained the three beautiful colours called rose-purple, violet-purple, and hyacinth-purple.

Q. Do not different countries adopt different colours for mourning?

A. Yes; in Europe the ordinary colour for mourning is *black*; in China it is *white*, a colour which was the mourning of the ancient Spartan and Roman ladies. In Turkey it is *blue* or *violet*; in Egypt, *yellow*; in Ethiopia, *brown*; and kings and cardinals mourn in *purple*.

Q. Does not every nation give a particular reason for the particular colour they assume in mourning?

A. Yes; *black,* which is the privation of light, indicates the privation of life; *white* is an emblem of the purity of the spirit, separated from the body; *yellow* is to represent, that death is the end of all our earthly hopes, because this is the colour of leaves when they fall, and flowers when they fade.

Q. What does *brown* denote?

A. The earth to which the dead return; *blue* is an emblem of happiness, which it is hoped the dead enjoy; and *purple* or *violet* expresses a mixture of sorrow and hope.

Q. Are not colours in China emblematical of rank?

A. Yes; *yellow* is the imperial colour for the emperor and his sons; *purple* for his grandsons; *red* is the symbol of virtue, truth, and sincerity; the emperor writes his edicts in *vermillion*; *black* denotes guilt and vice; *white,* moral purity.

Q. What different materials are used to obtain colours?

A. Some are obtained from woods, as Brazil wood affords red; logwood, purple; woad and indigo, blue dyes; and the saffron flower, yellow.

Q. What is indigo?

A. A beautiful blue dye, prepared from the fluid or pulp of an annual plant, which is cultivated with great care in the East and West Indies, and other parts of Asia and America.

Q. What is stone-blue, used by laundresses?

A. It is a preparation of indigo.

Q. What is woad?

A. A plant which grows wild in Cambridgeshire, Somersetshire, and Durham; the leaves are picked, ground, and reduced to a pulp, and formed into little balls, and exposed to the sun to dry.

Q. Is not this plant believed to be the same used by the Britons to stain and paint their bodies with?

A. Yes; and the *genet* of the French is a species of the same plant; this is famous for having been the badge of a long line of English kings hence called *Plantagenet*.

Q. What is weld?

A. A plant, like mignonette, used in dyeing, cultivated in England : it imparts to wool, cotton, and silk, a very bright yellow.

Q. What is alkanet ?

A. The bark of a root used in dyeing ; it imparts a fine deep red colour to all unctuous substances.

Q. Is it cultivated in England ?

A. But little ; it is principally imported from the neighbourhood of Montpellier in France, and from the Levant.

Q. What is verditer ?

A. A preparation of copper ; sometimes used by painters for a blue colour, but often mixed with a yellow to make a green.

Q. In the process of dyeing, must not every substance be prepared before it receives the colour ?

A. Yes, or it would wash out ; this preparation is called mordant ; alum is good for linens and cottons, and solutions from metals for silk and wool.

Q. Must the article to be dyed be dipped in this mordant first?

A. Yes; and well dried before it is put into the colouring liquor.

Q. What great good does this mordant effect?

A. It firmly fixes the colour, and gives it great brilliancy.

Q. What is alum?

A. A very valuable salt, obtained from ores, or from clay or earths, containing sulphur, dug out for this purpose.

Q. What part of the world has the merit of this useful discovery?

A. The East; but since the reign of Queen Elizabeth it has been prepared and made in Europe.

Q. Why is it reckoned so very valuable?

A. Because it is used in so many manufactures, in dyeing, and tanning, also in preparing paints, in making candles to harden them, in making paper, by wine merchants to fine their wine, and by bakers to whiten bread.

Q. Who introduced it into England?

A. Sir Thomas Chaloner, in 1595, who, during his travels in Italy, discovered that the mineral from which it was made was the same as one which abounded on his own estate at Whitby.

Q. Had it not been for several ages a monopoly in the hands of the court of Rome?

A. Yes; and so jealous were they of it, that it is said, when he had engaged a number of the Pope's workmen to accompany him to England, he was obliged to have them conveyed on ship-board concealed in large casks.

Q. Do not some insects yield a fine dye?

A. Yes; both cochineal and gum-lac.

Q. What is cochineal?

A. A very beautiful scarlet dye, produced from insects about the size of a small pea, which are only found in Mexico and New Spain.

Q. How are they procured?

A. The cochineal insects adhere in great numbers in a torpid state to the leaves of a prickly pear; at a certain time of the year they are carefully picked or brushed off by an instrument in the form of a pen.

Q. Is not this a very tedious operation?

A. Yes; the persons employed in it are sometimes obliged to sit for hours beside a single plant.

Q. How does the cochineal appear in this country?

A. In the form of a reddish shrivelled grain covered with a white bloom or powder: the male has wings, the female not.

Q. Will cochineal of itself produce such a brilliant colour?

A. No; it gave at first only a dull crimson colour, until a chemist of the name of Kuster discovered the art of preparing it with a solution of tin.

Q. What is carmine?

A. Only a preparation of cochineal.

Q. What is gum-lac?

A. A resinous colouring substance like wax, produced by the punctures of a species of ant, a native of the East Indies. The best lac is of a deep red colour.

Q. Where do these insects abound?

A. They are found upon trees on both sides of the river Ganges, in India; the only trouble in getting them is to break down the branches of the trees, and carry them to market.

Q. Are seed-lac and shell-lac the produce of the same insect as gum-lac?

A. Yes; it is only differently prepared, and is much used in painting, dyeing, sealing-wax, and varnish.

Q. What is varnish?

A. A compound of gum, mixed with spirits of wine and other ingredients, laid upon wood, metal, and other bodies, to make them shine; also used for setting a gloss upon cabinets, pictures, &c.

Q. What is the fine black varnish so much used in China and Japan?

A. The resinous juice of the Tseih-shoo shrub: it is poisonous in its liquid state, and requires the greatest caution in using: whatever it touches it stains of a deep black colour.

Q. How is this precious varnish collected?

A. When the shrubs that yield it are seven or eight years old, incisions are made in their bark, under which they force the edge of a shell, into which during the night the varnish flows.

Q. Is not this process repeated every night?

A. Yes, during the summer, until the varnish ceases to flow. It is computed that fifty trees will yield a pound of varnish every night.

Q. What is japanning?

A. The art of painting and varnishing ornaments on wood, metals, leather, and paper prepared for the purpose.

Q. Why is it called japan?

A. Because the first pieces of this beautiful ware which were brought to England came from Japan and China.

Q. Where is Japan?

A. In Asia; it is a large country, composed of several islands in the North Pacific Ocean, very rich in gold, and noted for many curious customs.

Q. Mention some of these.

A. We uncover the head out of

respect, and they the feet: we are fond of white teeth, and they of black: we get on horseback on the left side, and they on the right.

Q. What is peculiar in their domestic arrangements?

A. They never use any chairs, tables, or bedsteads.

Q. What do the Japanese principally trade in?

A. Gold, silver, cabinets, and other japan and lacquered wares; but the Dutch and Chinese were the only people with whom until recently they held any intercourse.

Q. Did not the late Lord Elgin conclude a treaty in 1858 which will sanction commercial dealings with this intelligent people?

A. Yes; and we have received wonderful accounts of their civilization.

Q. Who has recently written an interesting narrative of the manners and customs of the Japanese?

A. Sir Rutherford Alcock; as envoy of the Queen he resided for three years at Yeddo, the chief city of Japan.

Q. Are there not two Emperors?

A. Yes; one of them, called the Mikado, never quits his palace at Miaco, and his authority appears to be nominal.

Q. What is the other Emperor called?

A. The Tycoon, and he seems to exercise considerable authority.

Q. But is not the chief power of the state vested in the nobility?

A. Yes; they are called the Daimios, and number about three hundred and sixty: many of them keep thousands of armed retainers, and are very wealthy.

Q. Is not the scenery of Japan very beautiful?

A. Yes; and with the exception perhaps of England no country is so highly cultivated.

Q. Are not the Japanese deceitful in their dealings with foreigners?

A. They are so: and since Lord Elgin's treaty many outrages have been committed upon the English residents at Yeddo.

Q. Do not the French, and especially the English, imitate the art of japanning so well as to render the trade in japan ware of comparatively little consequence ?

A. Yes; Pontypool, Birmingham, and London, are famous for their tea-trays, dressing-boxes, cabinets, and snuff-boxes.

Q. What is paint?

A. A mixture of oil and colours, so various, according to the style of painting designed, that it is impossible to describe them.

Q. Who invented painting in oil colours ?

A. John Van Eyk, in Henry the Fifth's time; he discovered, accidentally, that his colour mixed better with oil than with water, and he excelled in producing a rich colouring.

Q. Whose oil paintings are some of the earliest known to us?

A. Those of Mabuse and Holbein. Henry VIII. patronized the latter, and once said to a nobleman, who was irritated against him, " I can when I please make seven lords of seven ploughmen :

but I cannot make one Holbein even of seven lords."

Q. What is the meaning of painting in enamel?

A. It signifies the laying on of mineral colours upon gold, silver, copper, &c.; the purest gold is the best, because it receives all colours.

Q. How are the colours applied?

A. They are reduced to a very fine powder, some mixed with oil of spike, and some with water, and laid on like other paints, but their brilliancy is not apparent till they have been baked in a little furnace, when their lustre is most beautiful, and no length of time changes them.

Q. Is it not an expensive process?

A. Certainly, and is consequently confined to miniatures, and small articles. The art is very ancient, and has been carried to great perfection by the French.

Q. What is fresco-painting?

A. Painting executed in water colours on wet plaster.

Q. Has this splendid art been long known?

A. Yes; it is coeval with architecture; fresco-paintings have been found in Egypt, Mexico, and India, which must have been executed 2000 years B.C., and yet retain all their original brilliancy.

Q. By what methods is this accomplished?

A. Through a long and tedious preparation applied to the wall, on which the painting is to be done, occupying two or three years; the mortar must be thoroughly wet when the painter begins his picture, so that the first tints laid on sink in and look faint, and must be repeated till the full effect is produced.

Q. How is this effected, for can he do a painting in a day?

A. In this way: not more is wetted than the painter can finish, and every defect in the first operation is irretrievable, the spoiled part must be cut out, and the process of preparation repeated for that part, but when completed it is very durable unless injured by damp.

Q. What European countries boast of the finest fresco-paintings?

A. Italy, Rome, Venice, Genoa, and Florence possess some of the most splendid; and Munich is now cultivating this art with great care and labour.

Q. What is oil of spike?

A. An essential oil distilled from lavender, much used by varnish-makers and the painters in enamel.

Q. What is mezzotinto?

A. A particular manner of engraving, by representing figures on copper so as to form prints in imitation of painting in Indian ink.

Q. Who invented it?

A. Prince Rupert usually has the credit; but it is supposed he learned the secret from a Colonel de Siegan, and brought it to England in the reign of Charles the Second.

Q. Who was Siegan?

A. An officer in the service of the Landgrave of Hesse.

Q. Who excel in this method of engraving?

A. The English.

Q. What is gilding?

A. Gold laid on any surface by way of ornament.

Q. How is this wonderful operation performed?

A. A bar of gold is made red-hot and beaten till it becomes as thin as paper: it is then divided into equal square pieces, and again forged or heated.

Q. What other process is necessary?

A. These squares are interlaid with leaves of vellum, and the gold beaten with the heaviest hammer, till it is stretched to the extent of the vellum.

Q. What follows?

A. These pieces of vellum are now crossed with leaves made of the gut of an ox properly prepared, five inches square, and the gold is again beaten, till it is stretched to the size of the pieces of skin.

Q. Is this the whole of the operation?

A. Yes; nothing remains but cutting

P

the edges even, and fixing the leaves of gold in books, the paper of which is well smoothed and prepared, that they may not stick to them.

Q. Is the gold-beater's skin which is used for healing cuts the same which you have just mentioned as prepared from the gut of an ox?

A. Yes.

Q. What is printing?

A. The art of making an impression upon one body, by pressing it with another, leaving the characters or figures on paper, linen, silk, &c.

Q. What is the common story about the invention of printing?

A. It is said Laurentius Coster, of Haarlem, diverted himself with cutting letters on the bough of a birch-tree, and the thought struck him to take the impression off on paper with ink.

Q. But did not two of his servants steal his types?

A. Yes; and they fled to Mainz, where under John Faust they pretended to be the first inventors of printing.

Q. Is there not an old parchment of Coster's still preserved in Germany?

A. Yes; it has the alphabet and the Lord's prayer printed on it.

Q. How many kinds of printing are there?

A. Several; it is an art daily improving; one method is from moveable letters; another by solid pages, casts of the above, called stereotype.

Q. What are they used for?

A. The printing of books and newspapers.

Q. Were newspapers the immediate result of the invention of printing?

A. No; the first newspaper was printed in London, in 1622, by Nathaniel Butter; it was called the *Weekly News*, being published generally every week.

Q. Did it meet with much success?

A. No; and after some years was discontinued; for unfortunate writers were at that time often cruelly punished for merely expressing opinions on political matters.

Q. When did newspapers first show literary merit?

A. In the reign of Queen Anne, when Dean Swift, Addison, and Steele were contributors.

Q. Was not the reign of this queen celebrated for its great writers?

A. Yes; so that it has been called *the golden age* of our literature.

Q. What is the most wonderful newspaper in the world?

A. The *Times*, of which about sixty thousand copies are now printed everyday.

Q. By what means?

A. By Applegath's steam-press, which strikes off 160 copies in a minute.

Q. How are pictures printed?

A. From copper or steel plates, or from wooden or stone blocks, on which the picture is beautifully engraved or drawn.

Q. How are linens, calicos, &c., printed?

A. From blocks of copper, wood, or stone, on which are cut birds, flowers, or any other fancy patterns.

Q. What is drawing on stone called?

A. Lithography; it is of recent invention, and found to be very useful in ornamenting books, and various other things.

Q. Cannot the electric telegraph now print the messages which are sent by it?

A. Yes; and by this extraordinary discovery a message can be sent any distance in a second of time.

Q. How?

A. By means of electricity conducted by wires.

Q. In what manner does this convey information?

A. A dial plate is connected with each end of the wire, and when the needle is moved by a person on one dial, the current of electricity almost immediately moves the needle in a similar way at the other extremity.

Q. When was this extraordinary invention first brought into use?

A. In 1837, by Professor Wheatstone.

Q. Has not the electric telegraph

P 3

been successfully carried under the sea?

A. Yes; from Dover to Cape Grisnez, near Calais. The wire is coated with gutta percha, and so kept dry. The first communication by means of it was on August 28th, 1850.

Q. Is there not at the present time a submarine electric telegraph between England and Ireland?

A. Yes; it was first used January 16th, 1854.

Q. Was not the telegraph laid under the Atlantic Ocean in 1858?

A. Yes; from Valentia in Ireland, to Trinity Bay, Newfoundland, but after a few weeks the cable became useless.

Q. What cities dispute the honour of giving birth to the men who claim the merit of the invention of printing?

A. Mainz, Haarlem, and Strasburg; it is generally thought the first attempts at printing with moveable types were made in the latter city by John Guttemburg, a native of Mainz.

Q. But is it not generally conceded

that Laurentius Coster of Haarlem first invented the art of producing impressions from fixed blocks of type?

A. Yes; but by this process the type could, of course, only be used for one book.

Q. By whom was this invaluable art introduced into England?

A. By William Caxton, a merchant of London, who acquired the art during his travels abroad.

Q. What age was he when he taught his countrymen this useful and beautiful art?

A. Fifty-seven; he resided some years at Cologne, for the purpose of learning it, and printed above fifty different books before he died.

Q. In what city of England did Caxton establish the first printing-press?

A. At Westminster, where it is said the first book he printed was on the game of chess.

Q. Is there not some doubt if Caxton did really introduce printing into England?

A. Yes; about two hundred years after Caxton's time a book was dis-covered which bore date at Oxford, in 1468, which was three years before the commencement of Caxton's labours.

Q. Did not this question at one time divide the literary world to a violent degree?

A. Yes; and the result of the dis-putation appears to show that Caxton was the first who printed in England with *metal* types, but that a workman from Haarlem, named Corsellis, had previously printed with wooden ones, at Oxford.

Q. Were not even the higher classes very uneducated during the middle ages?

A. Yes; and even as late as the reign of Edward VI. there were peers of parliament unable to read.

Q. Who were the best educated per-sons at the early periods of our history?

A. The ecclesiastics and monks; and this was one reason of their great power and influence.

Q. Did not the late Monsieur Daguerre discover a beautiful method of taking likenesses ?

A. Yes, in the year 1839; and the art is called " *daguerreotype* " after his name.

Q. How were these likenesses taken ?

A. Upon plates of copper covered with silver, which was washed with a solution of nitric acid.

Q. What was the next process?

A. The plate was placed in a kind of camera-obscura, and the impression of the object was then subjected to the action of mercury, and afterwards washed in distilled water, whereby it became perfectly fixed.

Q. What is the great merit of daguerreotypes?

A. Their perfect accuracy of outline; but for many years the objects taken by this process had a dark, unpleasing appearance.

Q. Has not this defect been overcome by the improved art of photography ?

A. Yes ; and portraits are now

coloured as beautifully as miniatures painted entirely by the hand.

Q. Has not the process been recently applied in copying the drawings and paintings of the old masters?

A. Yes; and the celebrated cartoons of Raphael at the Kensington Museum have been photographed in a manner which excels the finest engraving.

Q. Are not great improvements being constantly made in this beautiful art?

A. Yes; and landscapes, buildings, and almost every kind of object are now taken.

Q. Who is said to have invented chess?

A. Ulysses. William the Conqueror, King John, and Charles I., were doatingly fond of this scientific game.

Q. Do not printers use a peculiar kind of ink?

A. Yes; it is like paint, and is applied to the printing-types by means of balls and rollers.

Q. How is this ink made?

A. From burnt linseed oil mixed with lamp-black.

Q. Does it not dry very quickly?

A. Yes; without running through to the other side, or blotting the letters.

Q. You have mentioned chess: pray is backgammon a very old game?

A. Yes; it was played by the Saxons and Danes when in possession of England.

Q. By whom is it said to have been invented?

A. By the Welsh, and called by them from two words in their language, "back cammon," or *a little battle*.

Q. Is it not also a genuine Saxon compound word?

A. Yes; *bac*, or *baec*, and *gamen*, meaning *back-game*, so called because the game consists in the players bringing back their men from their opponents' tables into their own; and when their pieces are taken up, being obliged to go back.

Q. Which is the most ancient game still in common practice?

A. Draughts: Rameses, the king of Egypt, is represented on the walls of his palace at Thebes engaged in the game of draughts.

Q. What is Indian ink?

A. An ink used in drawing, brought from China, in small oblong cakes, which, on being dipped into water, and rubbed, make a most beautiful black.

Q. How is it made?

A. It is supposed to be made of fine lamp-black, and another substance like glue.

Q. Is there no other idea about this secret?

A. Yes; the cuttle-fish is furnished with a vessel which contains a quantity of dark inky fluid, and many think the Chinese make Indian ink of this, perfumed with musk and other things.

Q. What is lamp-black?

A. A soot prepared by burning the dregs and coarser parts of tar in furnaces; the smoke is carried through tubes into boxes covered with linen, upon which it settles.

Q. What is then done?

A. The soot is carefully beaten off

into boxes, and afterwards packed in barrels for sale.

Q. What is it principally used for?

A. Printing and dyeing: it received its name from formerly being made by means of lamps.

Q. What is ivory-black?

A. Burnt ivory, or bones, which becoming quite black, and reduced to thin shavings, are ground in water to powder.

Q. Who make great use of it?

A. Both painters and jewellers.

Q. Is there not a peculiar ink used for copper plates?

A. Yes; it is a composition made of the stones of peaches and apricots, the bones of sheep, and ivory, all well burnt, and called *Frankfort black*, mixed with nut oil that has been well boiled, and ground together on a marble.

Q. How is this ink used?

A. They take a small quantity of it on a rubber made of linen rags, and smear the whole face of the plate as it lies on a grate, over a charcoal fire: they then first wipe it over with a rag, then with the palm of each hand.

Q. Does not the address of the workman consist in wiping the plate perfectly clean without taking the ink out of the engraving?

A. Yes. The plate thus prepared is laid on the board of the press; over the plate is laid the paper, first well moistened to receive the impression, and over the paper two or three folds of flannel.

Q. What follows?

A. It is passed through between the rollers, which, pinching very strongly, yet equally, press the moistened paper into the strokes of the engraving, whence the ink is transferred to the paper.

Q. What is lime?

A. It is a substance found in spars, shells, stone, marble, and chalk; it becomes lime by being burnt for a long time, after which it is called quick-lime.

Q. What is its principal use?

A. To make mortar; it is also useful in agriculture as a manure to fertilize land, and in several manufactures.

Q. What are bricks?

A. They are made of a rich yellowish earth or clay, well mixed or prepared, then called loam.

Q. How are they formed?

A. In wooden moulds, and are dried by being placed in the open air.

Q. Are they then fit for building?

A. No; they must be piled up into square heaps, with cinders and straw between each brick to keep them hot, and then burnt.

Q. How long will they require burning?

A. Two or three weeks to do them thoroughly.

Q. What are these square heaps of bricks called?

A. Clamps; but the best bricks are burnt in kilns, by means of a hot furnace beneath them.

Q. Who first taught his subjects to make bricks?

A. King Alfred.

Q. When used for buildings, how are they joined together?

A. By mortar.

Q. What is mortar?

A. It is made by mixing lime, sand, and cut horse or ox hair, with water; this mortar is used for plastering.

Q. What is the difference betwixt that and what is used for cement?

A. No hair is used in the latter.

Q. What are tiles?

A. A sort of thin brick, made of clay, moulded of a certain thickness, dried, and burnt in a kiln.

Q. What are slates?

A. A sort of stone which splits into thin plates, and is used for covering buildings instead of tiles.

Q. How are they fastened to the roof?

A. By pegs driven through them, and they are made to lap over each other at the edges, in order to keep out the rain.

Q. Where are slates chiefly obtained?

A. From Carnarvonshire and Lancashire, and Argyleshire in Scotland; there are quarries of inferior magnitude in Westmoreland, and other parts of the country.

Q. How are writing slates made ?

A. A solid dark-coloured slate is chosen, which is split and smoothed with an iron instrument.

Q. Is this all that is done ?

A. No: they are ground with sandstone, slightly polished with tripoli, and lastly rubbed with charcoal powder.

Q. Are they now ready for use?

A. Yes; when they have been cut into the requisite shape, and set into a wooden frame.

Q. Are there no pencils for writing on these slates?

A. Yes; they are made of a particular soft slate, which falls into long splintery fragments.

Q. Is it not a business to form them into the requisite shape?

A. Yes; they are split by a particular instrument.

Q. Who principally use writing slates?

A. Young persons, to cypher on.

Q. By whom were the figures 1, 2, 3, &c., introduced into Europe ?

A. By the Saracens; and arithmetic

was considered so complex in the time of the Saxons in England, that it was said to be a study *too difficult for the mind of man.*

Q. What is tripoli?

A. A kind of clay of an earthy texture; formerly brought into Egypt from Tripoli, in Africa, but it is now found in many parts of Germany.

Q. What is its use?

A. It is valued for the polishing of metals and stones mixed with sulphur.

Q. Is not what we call rotten-stone a kind of tripoli?

A. Yes; it is dug in Derbyshire and Staffordshire, and is used for most of the purposes of tripoli.

Q. What is whitening?

A. A pounded chalk.

Q. What is putty?

A. It is made of whitening and linseed oil, well mixed together.

Q. What are flints?

A. Hard stones, found in pieces of different sizes, and commonly among chalk.

Q. What are they principally used for?

A. To burn into powder to mix with clays in making china, and, instead of sand, to melt into glass.

Q. Have they not become very valuable in making the finest roads?

A. Yes; by being broken into very small pieces they form a road as hard as a rock.

Q. Are not walls, and sometimes houses, built of flints?

A. Yes.

Q. Were not our roads in a very bad state before the present century?

A. Yes; and frequently impassable, except for travellers on horseback.

Q. Who invented the plan of making roads from flints or granite, broken into small pieces?

A. The late Mr. McAdam, and the process is usually called "*macadamizing*," after his name.

Q. Are gun-flints now used?

A. No; they have been superseded by percussion gun-caps, which discharge the gun with more certainty than flints.

Q. When were guns first generally used?

A. Not until the reign of Henry VIII.; and the first cannon-foundry was established in England in the first year of Mary's reign.

Q. Was not the idea of the trigger of the gun taken from the catch of the cross-bow?

A. Yes; it is formed on the same principle.

Q. Which is the first ship on record having port-holes in her sides for guns?

A. The *Great Harry*, or *Henry Grace à Dieu*, built by Henry VIII., at Woolwich, the most ancient dock-yard in England.

Q. Was she not the largest and most splendid vessel that had ever floated on the Atlantic?

A. Yes; and she had four masts, a very uncommon thing at that time, as most vessels had but one.

Q. Did she carry cannon?

A. Yes; eighty guns and a crew of 700 men.

Q. What became of this fine ship?

A. It was burned in the dock-yard of Woolwich, owing to the carelessness of its crew.

Q. What did they shoot from their guns and cannons in those days?

A. Stones, instead of iron bullets, which was an improvement afterwards found out.

Q. What are galleys?

A. They are decked vessels with a great number of oars.

Q. Is it not very laborious work to row these galleys?

A. Yes; abroad it was commonly made a punishment for criminals, who were chained to their benches, and could not escape: this mode of punishment is now discontinued.

Q. What is Portland stone?

A. It is a stone obtained from a mass of rocks, named the Isle of Portland, in Dorsetshire.

Q. What is Portland stone generally called?

A. Free-stone, because it does not split as some do, but may be freely cut any way.

Q. Does not this render it one of the best stones for building?

A. Yes; besides which, on its being exposed to the air, it becomes hard and beautifully white.

Q. What public buildings in London are built of it?

A. Some of the bridges, St. Paul's Cathedral, the Monument, Whitehall, &c. After the great fire of London, Sir Christopher Wren brought it into general use.

Q. What other place in Dorsetshire is noted for its stone quarries?

A. Purbeck, near Portland: the stone is very useful for paving the broad foot-paths in the streets.

Q. How many churches did Sir Christopher Wren build in London?

A. Fifty-eight: of these St. Paul's is his greatest work.

Q. How long was it building?

A. Thirty-five years; Sir Christopher died in 1710, the year it was finished, aged ninety.

Q. What does the Monument commemorate?

A. The fire of London: it is erected near the spot where it first broke out, and directly opposite to it once stood the house of the Black Prince.

Q. What is its height?

A. 202 feet, and St. Paul's is 404.

Q. Where was the first stone church erected in England?

A. At Lincoln, and it was thought a great curiosity.

Q. Who built Westminster Hall?

A. William Rufus: it was one of the largest rooms in Europe supported without a pillar; he also built the Tower of London.

Q. What is remarkable of the death of this king?

A. That being at dinner with Sir Walter Tyrrel, before he went out hunting, he desired some arrows to be brought him, and picking out six very long and sharp ones, he gave two of them to Sir Walter, saying, "You are a good marksman, and know how to use them."

Q. Was it by one of these arrows he was shot?

A. Yes; in the New Forest in Hampshire.

Q. How much did Henry VII. expend in building the superb chapel called after him at Westminster?

A. 20,000*l.*; a very large sum in those days.

Q. Was not the skill of foreign artists employed in this master-piece of architecture?

A. Yes; and Torrigiano, a Florentine of some note, is said to have erected the king's tomb, which excites the admiration of modern architects.

Q. Were not some of the finest Gothic buildings we have built in the reign of Henry III.?

A. Yes; the carved work of all kinds was most elaborate, and the outsides were adorned with pinnacles and lofty steeples.

Q. Could such curious buildings be erected by common workmen?

A. No; a number of the best artificers formed themselves into a company, and went about from place to place as they were wanted.

Q. What did they call themselves?

A. Free-masons; and this is by some considered the origin of the famous society of Free-masons, though others attribute to them a much higher antiquity.

Q. Who was the celebrated carver in wood in James the Second's time?

A. Gibbons; some of the finest specimens of his festoons and flowers are to be seen at Windsor, and at Petworth in Sussex.

Q. What is granite?

A. A valuable stone, noted for its hardness and durability: it is abundant in Cornwall and Devonshire, as well as in the county of Aberdeen in Scotland, and forms the summits of most of the highest mountains in the world.

Q. What are its uses?

A. The carriage way of the streets of London is paved with it on account of its strength: public building steps, and other things are made of it.

Q. Has the weather any effect upon it?

A. Very little: and this induced the proprietors of Waterloo Bridge to use it for that noble structure; it was also used for the new London Bridge.

Q. Who built the first stone bridge?

A. The Empress Maud, or Matilda, the daughter of Henry I., at Stratford-le-bow, near London.

Q. In whose reign was the old London Bridge built, which was removed in 1831?

A. In that of King John; the former one was of wood.

Q. Where are millstones for grinding corn found?

A. Chiefly at Andernach, near Coblentz on the Rhine, where there are several quarries of stone harder even than granite.

Q. Is not the Temple Church, London,

well worth the attention of the curious?

A. Yes; it was built by the Knights Templars after the model of that of the Holy Sepulchre; it is curious from its antiquity, architecture, and the monuments of some of the old knights.

Q. Were not great honours allowed to all knights who returned from the holy wars?

A. Yes; and at their death they were privileged to have their figures represented with their legs crossed on their tombs.

Q. What do you mean by gems?

A. Precious stones.

Q. Which are esteemed the most valuable gems?

A. The diamond, ruby, emerald, and sapphire; then the amethyst, topaz, and aqua-marine, are considered of equal value; and the garnet is the cheapest.

Q. What is the peculiar property of the diamond?

A. It is the hardest and most brilliant of all natural productions, and can only be cut and polished by its own powder.

Q. What did the ancients call it?

A. Adamant; and all the precious stones were known to them by the same names we call them.

Q. In what holy book are all these stones enumerated?

A. In the Bible; they formed the breast-plate of Aaron, the high priest.

Q. What was this breast-plate called?

A. The Urim and Thummim: these mean *light* and *perfection*.

Q. What was engraved on each of these stones?

A. The name of one of the tribes of Israel; they declared the pleasure of the Almighty by shining brilliantly, or appeared dull when He disapproved.

Q. Who taught the Israelites the art of working gold and precious stones?

A. God Himself, who inspired one of the tribe of Judah with the knowledge of cutting stones, setting in gold and silver, and carving in wood.

Q. Where are diamonds found?

A. The best come from the East Indies: but they are also found in Borneo, and in several parts of South America.

Q. Which are the principal mines?

A. Those of Raolconda and Coulour, in the province of Golconda, formerly part of the Mogul's empire; and that of Soumelpour, or Goval, in Bengal.

Q. Where was the Mogul's empire?

A. In Hindostan, in Asia: it now belongs to England.

Q. Pray when did the English first establish themselves in Hindostan or India?

A. In the year 1612, when a company of English merchants settled at Surat, about 150 miles north of Bombay.

Q. But when may it be said that the foundations of our empire over this immense country were first laid?

A. By the great victory of Lord Clive, won June 23rd, 1757, over the Nabob Surajah-Dowlah at Plassey, about 100 miles north of Calcutta.

Q. Who consolidated the British power?

A. Warren Hastings, who was appointed the first governor-general of India in 1772.

Q. What great general distinguished himself in India at an early age?

A. The late Duke of Wellington, then Sir Arthur Wellesley, who won the battle of Assaye, September 23rd, 1803.

Q. Have many additions been made to our empire since that time?

A. Yes: the most memorable are the conquest of Scinde, by the late General Sir Charles James Napier in 1843, and of the Punjaub by Lord Gough in 1846.

Q. Pray where are Scinde and the Punjaub situated?

A. On the north-western frontier of India.

Q. Is not the extent of India very great?

A. Yes; it is about fifteen times the size of Great Britain, and contains a population estimated at 200 millions.

Q. Are we not responsible as a nation for the well-being of this immense multitude?

A. Yes; God has made England the most powerful of all nations, and we ought, therefore, to govern with mercy and justice.

Q. Why?

A. Because if we do so, He will continue to bless and prosper us.

Q. What does India produce?

A. Rice, cotton, silk, flax, hemp, sugar, opium, tobacco, and many other things of which you will read in this book.

Q. But are its resources developed?

A. No; for at present but few railways have been constructed, so that the produce of the interior of the country cannot be exported.

Q. How are diamonds discovered?

A. By men who, by means of long iron rods, with hooks at the end, draw them out of the crevices of rocks, and afterwards wash them in tubs.

Q. Pray are they found bright?

A. No; they are covered with a thick earthy crust.

Q. How is this removed?

A. By polishing; the value of a diamond increases with its weight and colour.

Q. Who possesses the largest diamond ever known?

A. The King of Portugal; it weighs more than eleven ounces, and was found in Brazil; it is of very inferior quality.

Q. Has not a very large diamond been recently brought to England?

A. Yes; it is called Koh-i-noor, or the Mountain of Light, and was formerly in the possession of the Great Mogul.

Q. How did the English obtain it?

A. They took it from the Sikhs in the late war.

Q. Where was it found?

A. In the celebrated mines of Golconda, in 1550; just three centuries before its arrival in England.

Q. How much does it weigh?

A. Since it was re-cut in 1852 it

weighs only 102 carats; before then it weighed 279 carats; in its rough state it weighed nearly 800 carats.

Q. How much is it valued at?

A. Two millions sterling; until it was re-cut it was the largest one known, except that of the King of Portugal; and it is of the first water.

Q. What do you mean by a diamond being of the first water?

A. Being of superior quality.

Q. Has not the Emperor of Russia a large diamond?

A. Yes; it supports the eagle on the Russian sceptre; it weighs nearly 200 carats, and is about the size of a pigeon's egg.

Q. What story is told of this diamond?

A. It was once placed as the eye of an idol, in Seringham, in the Carnatic; a French grenadier contrived to become one of the priests to the idol, and stole it.

Q. What is the famous Pitt diamond?

A. It was a magnificent one purchased by a Mr. Thomas Pitt, and sold by him to the Regent Duke of Orleans for 135,000*l.* ; it weighed 130 carats.

Q. What is the weight of a carat ?

A. Between three and four grains.

Q. What was the value of the famous Pigot diamond ?

A. It was valued at 40,000*l.* ; and was disposed of by lottery many years ago.

Q. Who won it ?

A. A young man, who sold it at a low price. It was afterwards disposed of to the Pacha of Egypt for 30,000*l.*

Q. Whose sword of state did it afterwards ornament ?

A. Bonaparte's : it was recently in the possession of the late ex-King of the French.

Q. How long did the cutting of this diamond occupy?

A. Two years, and cost 3000*l.* ; and the fragments were worth several thousands.

Q. What account is there of the famous Sancy diamond?

A. Charles the Bold, Duke of Burgundy, was its first owner ; it was captured from him by the Swiss at the battle of Granson, in the year 1476.

Q. Who gives us this information?

A. Philip de Commines in his interesting Memoirs; he was prime minister of Louis XI., the powerful rival of Charles the Bold.

Q. To whom did this diamond afterwards belong?

A. To a French gentleman of the name of Sancy, who called it by his own name. Henry III. of France enjoined him to send the diamond to pledge it, but the servant entrusted with it, being attacked by robbers, swallowed it, and was murdered.

Q. How was it recovered?

A. Sancy ordered the corpse to be opened, and it was found in his stomach. Our James II. possessed it when he fled to France, and Louis XV. wore it at his coronation: it is of the first water, in the shape of a pear.

Q. Did not the Queen present a beautiful jewel to Miss Florence Nightingale?

A. Yes; as a token of her Majesty's gratitude to this excellent lady for her patriotic exertions in alleviating the sufferings of our brave soldiers during the Crimean war.

Q. Can you describe this jewel?

A. Yes; it is oval, the groundwork being white enamel, with a crimson cross, on which the royal initials and crown are set in diamonds.

Q. What appropriate inscription does it bear?

A. The words, "*Blessed are the merciful,*" are inscribed upon its black oval band.

Q. Is the diamond useful only as an ornament?

A. No; it is used by lapidaries for slitting hard stones; also for cutting and engraving other gems, and in the finer kind of clock-work, as well as cutting glass among glaziers.

Q. Whom do you mean by a lapidary?

A. It is his business to cut into shape and polish these gems, or precious stones, which is done by grinding them on a wheel with diamond powder.

Q. Does he set them?

A. No; this is the business of the jeweller, and requires great taste.

Q. What is the ruby?

A. A precious stone of a bright red colour.

Q. Where is it found?

A. In the sand of a certain river in Ceylon, and near the town of Sirian, the capital of Pegu.

Q. Where is Ceylon?

A. An island in the Indian Ocean.

Q. Where is Pegu?

A. A country to the east of the peninsular of India.

Q. What is the emerald?

A. A very rare gem of a dark green colour, brought also from Peru, in South America, and from parts of the East Indies.

Q. Where do most of the emeralds that are now brought to Europe come from?

A. They are obtained from a mine in

R

the valley of Muzo, near the mountains of New Granada, in South America.

Q. What was the size of the largest emerald mentioned?

A. It was as big as an ostrich's egg, and was worshipped by the Peruvians under the name of the Goddess, or Mother of Emeralds.

Q. Did they not bring the smaller ones as offerings to it?

A. Yes ; and the priests called them the daughters of the large one.

Q. What is a sapphire?

A. A beautiful gem of a fine blue colour, brought from the East Indies and the island of Ceylon, where it is found in the sands of the rivers.

Q. What is the amethyst?

A. The oriental amethyst is an extremely rare gem, of a rich purple colour.

Q. But what is the common amethyst which is chiefly seen?

A. It is a violet-coloured rock crystal, highly polished and transparent, cut into beautiful stones for necklaces, bracelets, ear-rings, &c.

Q. Where do they come from?

A. The most valuable from India and Ceylon, but the greater number from Brazil and Peru, in South America.

Q. Is there not a precious stone called the carbuncle?

A. Yes; it is a very beautiful gem, found only in the East Indies. Its colour is a deep red softened off into a strong scarlet.

Q. What is the topaz?

A. A gem of bright yellow colour, but there are orange, pink, and blue topazes.

Q. Where do the finest come from?

A. Brazil, Saxony, and many parts of Europe. Brazilian topazes, by being exposed to a great heat, become pink.

Q. Are they much valued?

A. No; they are too common to be thought much of by the lapidary or jeweller.

Q. What is the beryl, or aquamarine?

A. It is a stone of a light sea-green colour; the most beautiful are brought from the borders of China, and from Siberia and Brazil.

Q. What people hold the large ones in great esteem?

A. The Turks, who value them for the handles of their stilettos.

Q. Is not the garnet a very fine stone?

A. Yes; it is a gem of a dark crimson colour; the best are brought from Bohemia, where there are mines of them.

Q. Where is Bohemia?

A. A fine kingdom in Germany.

Q. What is the cairn gorum?

A. A stone obtained from a mountain of that name in the county of Aberdeen, in Scotland.

Q. Are they much in repute?

A. Yes; they are nearly as valuable as topazes, which they resemble, and if of a good colour, clear and large, they are sold at a high price for seals, necklaces, &c.

Q. What kind of gem is the onyx?

A. A partly transparent one, generally marked alternately with colours of white, black, brown, blue, and green, but none of red.

Q. Where is it found?

A. In the East Indies, Siberia, America, and Germany: the ancients attributed wonderful medicinal virtues to wearing the onyx.

Q. What does its name signify?

A. It is a Greek word signifying *a nail*, on account of its supposed resemblance in colour to the whitish crescent at the base of the human nail.

Q. What is the sardonyx?

A. A gem very similar to the onyx, only its stripes or bands of colour are more regular.

Q. By whom were these gems highly valued?

A. By the ancients, who engraved upon them, and made them into those beautiful cameos, many of which still ornament our cabinets.

Q. How is this done?

A. By their ingenuity in turning the natural veins and marks in the stones to the figures they engrave on them, so as to excite the greatest admiration.

Q. Are not cameos exquisitely carved out of a double stone, consisting of two distinct colours?

A. Yes; on which the lapidary engraves heads, or works out different representations according to his taste. Italy is the famous mart for them.

Q. Are not onyx cameos very expensive?

A. Yes; a very simple one will cost ten or twelve pounds.

Q. Is there not a cheaper kind of cameo made from shells?

A. Yes; they are chiefly manufactured in Paris: imitations are also frequently made of glass.

Q. What is the cornelian?

A. A stone in great request for seals, beads for necklaces, &c., usually of a red colour, though sometimes white, orange, or yellow.

Q. Where is it found?

A. In most countries; but the finest

come from India, and form a considerable branch of trade.

Q. What is chrysoprase?

A. A beautiful stone of a delicate apple-green colour, much prized by jewellers, brought from Silesia, in Germany.

Q. What are opals?

A. Half-transparent kinds of stone which have a milky cast, and when held betwixt the eye and light appear blue, green, red, and yellow.

Q. Are not seals of great antiquity?

A. Yes; they are often mentioned in the Bible, particularly *signets* or seal-rings, as engraving on gems was an art in which the ancients excelled; the seal has in all ages been attached to acts or deeds of importance.

Q. Where are these very beautiful stones obtained?

A. The principal opal mines in the world are those of Hungary; but they are found in other parts of Europe, and also in Sumatra and the East Indies.

Q. What is the turquoise?

A. A beautiful light blue substance, set in rings, &c.; they were very fashionable in all female ornaments.

Q. In what country are they very common?

A. In Persia; and the Turks value them highly, and constantly wear them in some part of their dress, and particularly to adorn the handles of their stilettoes.

Q. Where is there a mine of these stones?

A. At Nashabour, south of Meschid, in Persia.

Q. From what country are they brought into England?

A. From Russia; and they are stuck with pitch upon the ends of straws, because, if mixed, the purchaser would not so easily observe their colour, which is their chief value.

Q. Can they be easily imitated?

A. Yes, in paste; and they are often imposed upon the ignorant purchaser.

Q. What are pearls?

A. A hard, white, shining body, formed in the shell of a large oyster, or rather muscle, of which there are three kinds, having a beard growing out of them, thought to be caused by a distemper in the creature that produces them.

Q. Why?

A. Because the pearl-fishers say, that when the shell is smooth and perfect they never expect to find any pearls, but always do so when it has begun to be deformed and distorted.

Q. How can you account for this?

A. It would seem that as the fish grows older the vessels containing the juice for forming the shell, and keeping it in its vigour, become weak and ruptured, and thence, from this juice accumulating in the fish, the pearl is formed.

Q. Where do these oysters abound?

A. In the seas about the East Indies, and particularly in the Persian Gulf, and Ceylon; they grow on rocks, and are found in the deepest and stillest waters.

Q. How often does the fishery of Ceylon take place?

A. The same bank only once in seven years, which the oysters take to grow.

Q. Where are the richest pearls produced?

A. At Ormus, an island at the entrance of the Gulf of Persia.

Q. Are they easily obtained?

A. By no means; for these oysters lie at the bottom of the sea, and can only be got at by diving.

Q. How is this diving performed?

A. By men sinking themselves, by tying stones to their bodies, in the places where the fish are supposed to lie.

Q. What do they do when they reach the bottom?

A. They begin filling a bag of network, which is hanging about their necks, with the oysters; for they go down into the water with their eyes open.

Q. Do they not soon lose their breath?

A. It is rarely known for any diver

to hold it longer than fifty seconds. To aid him in retaining his breath, the diver places a piece of elastic horn over his nostrils, which binds them closely together.

Q. How do they get up when exhausted?

A. They pull a rope which is fastened to them, as a signal to their companions in the boat to draw them up.

Q. How often will the divers go down in a day?

A. Forty or fifty times, and at each plunge will return with about ten or twelve shells.

Q. Is not diving very injurious to health?

A. Yes; it shortens the lives of those who practise it much.

Q. Do not accidents frequently occur from sharks?

A. Not often; but the saw-fish is much dreaded by the divers of the Persian Gulf, where they have been completely cut in two by these monsters of the deep.

Q. How many pearls will one shell contain?

A. Sometimes a hundred, large and small; but often more than a hundred will be opened and not a single pearl of value will be found.

Q. How do they get the pearls out of the oysters?

A. When they have got a great many oysters, they are placed in heaps on the shore, covered with sand, where they continue about ten days.

Q. What does this cause?

A. The fish to decay and open, and the sand being sifted, the pearls are found.

Q. What is then done with them?

A. They are cleansed, polished, and bored, and washed in salt and water, to remove any stains.

Q. How is the value of pearls estimated?

A. By their size, roundness, colour, and brightness: it is a difficult task for the pearl-merchant to class them.

Q. Who says that pearls are the most excellent of all precious stones?

A. Pliny; and from our Saviour's comparing the kingdom of heaven to *a pearl of great price*, it would seem that they really were held in high estimation at that time.

Q. Which were the most renowned pearls ever mentioned?

A. The two which formed Cleopatra's ear-rings.

Q. What was the value of these two pearls?

A. It is recorded by Pliny, that the value of each was fifty-two thousand pounds sterling.

Q. What did she do with one, to transmit her boundless extravagance to posterity?

A. She gave an entertainment to her favourite, Mark Antony, which she declared should cost upwards of fifty thousand pounds.

Q. How did she contrive to expend this immense sum on one feast?

A. Every thing appeared to be very costly and magnificent, yet there was nothing which could cost that sum.

Q. What observation did Mark Antony make upon this?

A. He began to joke, when Cleopatra commanded him to be patient: "What you see," added she, "is only the first course."

Q. What did she mean?

A. She gave a signal, when two beautiful boys, richly dressed, brought her a magnificent vase studded with diamonds, which contained a strong vinegar.

Q. What use did she make of it?

A. The queen took from her ear one of her magnificent pearl ear-rings, and throwing it into the vase, watched with delight the gradual melting of this precious jewel : after which, gracefully drinking to the health of Mark Antony, she swallowed the costly draught.

Q. What became of the remaining pearl?

A. It was found among the treasures of which Augustus possessed himself, and was sawn in two for ear-rings for his daughter Julia.

Q. Was not this a proof that its equal could not be obtained?

A. Yes.

Q. But is there not another story respecting this famous pearl?

A. Yes; it was said to have been divided for the decoration of the image of Venus, the most perfect piece of sculpture of Praxiteles.

Q. What was this image celebrated for?

A. It was of marble, brilliantly white, and so entirely resembled life, that it appeared as if really animated.

Q. Who was Praxiteles?

A. A famous Grecian sculptor.

Q. Is there not a popular legend in our own country, which records a similar act of extravagance to Cleopatra's?

A. Yes; it is related that Sir Thomas Gresham, at the sumptuous banquet he gave Queen Elizabeth on the opening of the Royal Exchange, reduced to a powder a costly pearl, and mixing it in a goblet of wine, drank it to the health of his royal guest.

s 2

Q. What pearls do the English consider as most valuable?

A. Those brought from the fishery
of Ceylon.

Q. Are not pearls found in Great
Britain?

A. Yes; in the river Conway, in
Wales, and on the shores of the Tay,
and other parts of Scotland.

Q. Was there not a great fishery
of Scotch pearls carried on about
Perth?

A. Yes; but the avarice of the un-
dertakers quite exhausted it. They were
procured from the fresh-water muscle,
and from 1761 to 1764, 10,000*l.* worth
were sent to London, and sold from 10*s.*
to 1*l.* 16*s.* per ounce.

Q. What is mother-of-pearl?

A. The internal layer of the shell of
the pearl-oyster, and of other muscles of
the oyster kind.

Q. Is not this shell extremely brilliant
and smooth on the inside?

A. Yes; and it has the same lustre
on the outside, when the scales have

been cleared off by aqua-fortis and the lapidary's mill.

Q. What is its use?

A. It is made into snuff-boxes, handles for knives, buttons, spoons, fish and counters for card players, and is an article of great traffic with China.

Q. Where is this manufacture brought to great perfection?

A. At Jerusalem, where great quantities of this beautiful shell are procured from the Red Sea; most of the fine crucifixes and wafer boxes are made there.

Q. What are the beads called Roman pearls?

A. They are beads cut from thin plates of alabaster, and then dipped into a composition made of the scales of a fish called the argentina.

Q. Is not this imitation extremely good?

A. Yes; for they can copy the accidental defects of colour and form which occur in the real gem, as well as its brilliancy, so exquisitely as to deceive a practised eye.

s 3

Q. What is their great defect?

A. They are very heavy; for which reason glass has of late years to a considerable extent superseded the use of alabaster in their manufacture.

Q. Where is this most curious manufacture carried on?

A. At Rome, which is the reason of their being called Roman pearls.

Q. What is tortoise-shell?

A. The hard horny covering of the tortoise, used in inlaying, and in various other works, such as snuff-boxes, combs, &c.

Q. Does not the shell of the sea-tortoise afford a considerable article of exportation from the Seychelle Islands?

A. Yes; it abounds in these islands; for the female tortoise commonly deposits from ninety to one hundred eggs; she covers them with sand, and retires, leaving her progeny to be hatched by the piercing rays of the sun.

Q. Does she entirely forsake them?

A. No; allowing an interval of a few

days she returns a second and a third
time, and it is at this period she is taken,
by coming upon her suddenly and turning her on her back.

Q. How is the shell divided?

A. Into laminæ, or plates, of from
five to eight inches square.

Q. Where are the Seychelle Islands?

A. In the Indian Ocean, a few degrees north of the island of Madagascar.

Q. Pray what great king was nursed
in the shell of a tortoise?

A. Henry the·Fourth of France; the
cradle was long preserved in the castle
of Pau in the department of the Lower
Pyrenees, which was Henry's birth-
place.

Q. What else is still preserved there?

A. A huge steel two-pronged fork,
which was used by him, and thought a
most delicate invention.

Q. Were the ancients acquainted with
the use of forks?

A. No; it is quite certain that the
Greeks were ignorant of the use of forks
in eating, and it seems equally clear that

they were not used at table in any period of the Roman history.

Q. When does history record the first use of forks?

A. At the table of John the Good, Duke of Burgundy, and he had only two.

Q. How did they manage to carve without forks?

A. At that period the loaves were made round; they were cut into slices, which were piled by the side of the carver. He had a pointed carving-knife, and a skewer of gold or silver which he stuck into the joint; and having cut off a slice, he placed it on a piece of the bread which was served to the guest.

Q. Had not a leg or a haunch of mutton a piece of paper wrapped round the shank?

A. Yes; which the carver took hold of with the left hand when he carved the joint; this was the origin of our ornamenting hams with cut paper.

Q. When were forks introduced into this country?

A. Not generally till the time of James I., and it was thought a piece of affectation to use them in preference to fingers.

Q. Did not this dirty habit oblige all to wash before and after eating meat?

A. Yes.

Q. In the list of the plate of Queen Eleanor, the wife of Edward I., does there not occur an account of a pair of knives with silver sheaths, and a fork of crystal?

A. Yes; and also a silver fork handled with ebony and ivory, which proves our Plantagenet queens did not feed with their fingers at that time.

Q. But did not our ancient nobility live magnificently?

A. Yes; we read that the great Earl of Warwick, in the reign of Henry VI., gave an entertainment which lasted several days, at which 3500 persons were present.

Q. Is there not an account extant of the provision made by the earl for his guests?.

A. Yes ; it consisted of 300 quarters of wheat, 80 oxen, upwards of 1000 sheep, and other things in similar profusion.

Q. How are modern steel forks shaped ?

A. Upon an anvil, and the prongs are stamped out, tempered, and ground upon a dry stone.

Q. When is it considered by some persons that knives were first made in England ?

A. In the reign of Queen Elizabeth, by one Matthew, on Fleet Bridge.

Q. But is not this probably an error ?

A. Yes ; for knives of an inferior quality had for some centuries previous to that time been manufactured in the district about Sheffield, although the best were all imported from abroad until the reign of Queen Elizabeth.

Q. Is there not an European nation to whom the use of knives and forks in eating is still unknown ?

A. Yes ; the Turks never use them, and not even spoons except in eating soup.

Q. How many hands does a table-knife pass through before it is finished?

A. Sixteen hands in one hundred and forty-four stages of workmanship, which are so rapidly done, that at Sheffield a dinner knife is shaped in a few minutes.

Q. What is coral?

A. A beautiful branched substance, formed at the bottom of the sea by small animals called polypi, and it is their habitation.

Q. How many different kinds of coral are there?

A. Three; red, white, and black; the black is the rarest and most esteemed.

Q. What is coral like?

A. The red coral looks like branches of red sealing-wax.

Q. What is it principally used for?

A. To cut into beads for ornaments.

Q. Where is this wonder found?

A. In the Red Sea, between Asia and Africa, and in many parts of the Mediterranean, particularly about Marseilles, Tunis, and Sardinia.

Q. From what does the Red Sea derive its name?

A. Many have thought from its rocks of coral: but that is certainly not the only reason.

Q. What is the other?

A. The sea belonged to Esau, Jacob's brother, who was called Red from his hair being of that colour.

Q. Was it close to the country where he lived?

A. Yes; and that land was called Red land, and most probably the sea was also so named.

Q. Where is Marseilles?

A. A seaport of France, in Provence.

Q. Is there not white coral?

A. Yes; but it is of little value, and chiefly found on the shores of Ceylon.

Q. Have there not been many beautiful pieces of sculpture in coral?

A. Yes; the finest specimens known are a chess-board and men in the palace of the Tuileries at Paris.

Q. What is ivory?

A. The tusks and teeth of elephants;

the tusks are much longer in the male than in the female.

Q. What place produces the best?

A. The whitest, smoothest, and most compact ivory comes from Ceylon; it never turns a yellow.

Q. But is not ivory obtained from other animals besides the elephant?

A. Yes; from the hippopotamus, wild boar, &c.; but it is of an inferior kind.

Q. What is the great use of ivory?

A. For making boxes, dice, fans, handles of knives and forks, ornamented utensils, &c.

Q. What people excel in carving ivory?

A. The Chinese and Indians; their workmanship is exquisite. From a quantity of ivory not weighing more than 3lbs. they will make a toy worth a hundred dollars.

Q. Was not ivory highly valued by the ancients?

A. It appears so, for Homer speaks of the Trojans using it in adorning their bridles, which must be one thousand two hundred years before Christ.

Q. Is it not often named in the Bible?

A. Yes; particularly in the time of King Solomon, two hundred years after the Trojan war: his house, palace, bed, and vessels, were richly ornamented with or made of this costly material, brought at great labour and expense overland, or by a tedious coasting voyage by sea.

Q. What great master among the Greeks excelled in the working of ivory?

A. Phidias; . he made a statue of Minerva in gold and ivory thirty-nine feet in height, which was placed in the Parthenon at Athens: this splendid work raised Phidias many enemies, and caused him to be banished by a clamorous populace.

Q. To what place did he retire?

A. To Olympia, a town of Elis in the Peloponnesus, where he determined to revenge the ill-treatment he had received from his countrymen, by making a statue which should far excel his Minerva.

Q. Was he successful?

A. Yes; he made his Jupiter Olympius, sixty feet in height, which has passed for one of the wonders of the world, and it was considered a personal misfortune if any one died without seeing it.

Q. Where is the elephant found?

A. In both Asia and Africa; but the Asiatic elephant is by far superior in courage, docility, and intelligence, as well as in size, to the African species.

Q. How high is the Asiatic elephant?

A. Usually from nine to ten feet, with ears of a moderate size; the African rarely exceeds eight feet, having remarkably long ears spreading over the shoulders, and its countenance exhibits the same inferiority.

Q. Is not its strength immense?

A. Yes; far greater than that of any other quadruped; it can carry, on a journey, without any inconvenience, two thousand five hundred pounds, and can travel about fifteen leagues a day; its common pace is nearly the same as that of a horse walking, but it has a species of amble which is much quicker.

Q. Is it not exceedingly circumspect?

A. Yes; and it very seldom stumbles. In its wild state its age averages about 120 years; when domesticated, this term is much shortened from want of exercise, change of food, and its usual habits.

Q. Are there not white elephants?

A. Yes; they are objects of veneration and worship to some nations of the East, highly valued and coveted in all. The King of Siam had six of these animals.

Q. Are they rare?

A. Yes; this is the cause of their estimation: they are supposed to be the temporary habitation of the soul of some mighty personage in its progress to final perfection; therefore every white elephant has the rank or title of a king, such as the Pure King, the Wonderful King. The King of Siam never rides upon his, because he considers them as great as himself.

Q. Is not the finder of one of these rare creatures a most fortunate mortal?

A. Yes; he is rewarded with a crown of silver, and a grant of land equal in extent to the space of country at which the elephant's cry can be heard; he and his family are exempt from all sorts of servitude, and their land from taxation to the third generation.

Q. Were not elephants used in battle by the ancients?

A. Yes; but the Romans discovered that fire appalled them, and that they did more mischief to their own party than to the enemy.

Q. What is amber?

A. A substance usually of a golden yellow colour, found on the south coast of the Baltic, and also on the shores of Sicily, and the Adriatic.

Q. Is it not sometimes dug out of mines?

A. Yes; there is a fine mine in Prussia, and there is a gum so nearly like amber, that it can scarcely be distinguished from it.

Q. Is it exactly known what amber is?

A. No; but from the insects often found in it, it is supposed to have once been in a fluid state.

Q. What is eau-de-luce?

A. Oil of amber, mixed with sal-ammoniac.

Q. What is sal-ammoniac?

A. Salts formed from ammonia and muriatic acid, formerly brought from Egypt.

Q. From what did it derive its name?

A. From being found in great abundance among the sand near the temple of Jupiter Ammon, in Africa.

Q. How is it now made in Europe?

A. By burning at the same time soot, bones, oil, and salt, with other substances.

Q. Is it applied to many useful purposes?

A. Yes; it is used in medicine, and

by dyers to give brilliancy to many of their colours; also by copper-smiths and tinners, to clean the surface of metals, &c.

Q. What is sal-volatile?

A. An aromatic volatile salt, composed of sal-ammoniac, distilled with salt of tartar, softened with spirits of wine, and often scented with some essence.

Q. What is ambergris?

A. A substance found floating on the sea in warm climates, or thrown upon the shore; it is also taken from the inside of a particular kind of whale; its smell is extremely powerful.

Q. Whence does the best come?

A. From Madagascar and Java.

Q. What is it thought to be?

A. A disease of the fish.

Q. What is its use?

A. It was formerly used in medicine, but it is now chiefly used for a perfume.

Q. What is musk?

A. A strong perfume, found in a bag, about the size of a small egg, under the belly of an animal shaped like a deer, but without horns.

Q. Is it a valuable drug?

A. Yes; it is now chiefly used in medicine for spasms, convulsions, &c.; as a perfume it is too strong to be agreeable.

Q. Where is the musk animal found?

A. In Thibet, Tonquin, Siberia, and Bantam: they kill the animal, cut off the bags, and tie them closely up.

Q. Where is Bantam?

A. A large town in the island of Java.

Q. To whom does this island belong?

A. To the Dutch, who send a quantity of pepper and spices from it to all parts of the world every year.

Q. What is camphor?

A. It is a white resinous juice of a tree of the bay tribe, growing in China, Japan, and the islands of Sumatra, and Borneo.

Q. How is it procured?

A. In various ways: it is found in

every part of the trees, which are chopped into pieces and placed in covered iron vessels.

Q. What is then done?

A. The vessel is filled with rice-straw and rushes, and exposed to gradual heat, by which the camphor is extracted in a kind of vapour: this when cooled becomes condensed on the straws, which are then carefully removed.

Q. Does it not undergo a further process when brought to Europe?

A. Yes; it is refined by being mixed with a little lime and heated; the vapour thus produced becomes condensed when cool, and is then fit for use.

Q. Does every tree of the species yield this precious gum?

A. No; not a tenth of the trees which are destroyed yield any gum or oil.

Q. Is not camphor much used in medicine?

A. Yes: and its strong, delightful smell is so disagreeable to insects, that they always avoid it.

Q. Is it not also much used in perfumery?

A. Yes.

Q. Do not the Chinese make their coffins of camphor wood?

A. Yes; their habits differ from most other people; when a person dies, the body is put into a large coffin made of camphor wood, and remains in it till completely decomposed: it is then removed into an earthen jar with a cover, a small paper label, with the name of the deceased, being affixed to each.

Q. What is the otto of roses?

A. The oil of the flower whose name it bears.

Q. How is this charming scent procured?

A. By carefully distilling roses with water.

Q. What place is noted for the roses of which this expensive perfume is made?

A. Ghazeepoor on the Ganges, in India; the otto from this place gained the prize in the Great Exhibition of

1851, but Cannes, in the south of France, is also very celebrated for the manufacture.

Q. Has not the rose in all ages been more celebrated than any other flower?

A. Yes; for its beauty of form, delicacy of colour, and exquisite perfume, it has been represented as the emblem of beauty: and in ancient Rome, during public rejoicings, the streets were strewed with roses.

Q. Is not the art of preparing perfumes very ancient?

A. Yes; and in the reign of Queen Elizabeth noble ladies used to spend much of their time in this pursuit.

Q. Was not that queen very fond of perfumes?

A. Yes: Miss Strickland, in the Lives of the Queens of England, says that they were never richer, more elaborate, more costly, or more delicate, than in the reign of Elizabeth.

Q. Where do the plants chiefly flourish from which perfumes are obtained?

A. At the extensive flower-farms in the neighbourhood of Nice, at Montpellier, Nismes, Grasse, and Cannes in France, at Adrianople, and at Broussa in Asiatic Turkey.

Q. But where is the best lavender and peppermint produced?

A. At Mitcham in Surrey, and at Hitchin in Hertfordshire; they sell at a much higher price than the lavender and peppermint produced in France, or elsewhere.

Q. What is perhaps the most common kind of perfume?

A. Eau-de-Cologne; the best is made from spirit, rosemary, orange, citron, and bergamot.

Q. Is not that manufactured in this country inferior to the genuine perfume obtained at Cologne, and elsewhere on the Continent?

A. Yes; because we use spirit distilled from corn, but foreigners use *grape* spirit, which is much better adapted for the purpose.

Q. What two methods are chiefly

applied to extract perfumes from flowers and plants?

A. They are either submitted to great pressure, or are distilled by being placed in a vessel and subjected to heat.

Q. Are there not two other modes of process?

A. Yes; those called absorption and maceration: in the former a coarse cotton cloth is steeped in olive oil, and then laid upon a frame of wire gauze; on this the flowers are spread and left from 12 to 72 hours; they are then changed: the process of maceration is somewhat similar.

Q. What is the most lasting of all perfumes?

A. That called Frangipanni, from the name of a noble Roman, who invented it; the plant from which it is obtained flourishes in the West India Islands.

Q. How is lavender water made?

A. By filtering English oil of lavender, spirit, and rose-water.

Q. Do not the leaves of the geranium yield a delightful perfume?

T

A. Yes; and it so nearly resembles the real otto of roses, that it is often used to adulterate that most expensive perfume.

Q. Are there not also dry perfumes?

A. Yes; and these are the most ancient; they are now usually called sachet powders, from being put into small silk bags or ornamental envelopes: these perfumes are prepared by grinding flowers or herbs in a mill, or powdering them in a mortar, and they are afterwards sifted.

Q. What is myrrh?

A. A gum obtained by incision from a tree resembling the acacia; it grows on the eastern coast of Arabia Felix, and that part of Abyssinia near the Red Sea; also in the Levant, and the East Indies.

Q. Is it not reckoned a perfume, as well as a most valuable medicine?

A. Yes; it has an aromatic smell when burnt, and a bitter taste when taken into the stomach, which it warms and strengthens.

Q. Was it not one of the gifts offered by the wise men to our Saviour?

A. Yes; they presented to Him gold, frankincense, and myrrh.

Q. What did they mean by these offerings?

A. Gold signified Christ to be a king; myrrh being used in embalming the dead, to prevent putrefaction, signified He was to die; and the incense represented Him to be God.

Q. What is frankincense?

A. A gum, which upon the application of heat emits a most fragrant smell.

Q. Of what places is the tree a native?

A. Of Syria and Arabia.

Q. What is opium?

A. A gummy juice obtained by incisions from the head of the *papaver somniferum*, or white poppy.

Q. How is it prepared?

A. The poppy head, when green and full-grown, is wounded, and the juice is scraped off as it oozes out, and is put into earthen vessels, and worked about with the hand in the open sunshine.

Q. What does this effect?

A. It becomes of consistency sufficient to form into balls, cakes, &c., which are further dried.

Q. From whence is it brought?

A. It is imported from Persia, Arabia, India, and other warm parts of Asia, in flat cakes covered with poppy or tobacco leaves, to prevent them from sticking together.

Q. Is it not considered one of the most valuable medicines known?

A. Yes; it is chiefly used as a remedy for procuring sleep, and lessening pain, which it does in a most remarkable manner.

Q. Is it not also a deadly poison?

A. Yes: if taken in large doses.

Q. What people are passionately fond of it?

A. The Asiatics and the Turks.

Q. What is laudanum?

A. A liquid made from opium and spirits of wine.

Q. If accidentally taken, what is the best remedy?

A. To drink freely of acids and coffee, and not to yield to the desire of sleeping.

Q. What is chloroform ?

A. A liquid recently much used, as it throws persons who inhale it into a deep sleep, and renders them insensible to pain.

Q. How is it obtained?

A. By distilling a mixture of chloride of lime, spirits, and water.

Q. What is tobacco?

A. The dried leaves of a beautiful annual plant, which requires great care in the cultivation.

Q. Where does it grow?

A. In many parts of North America, and in the West Indies.

Q. From which of the islands did it receive its name?

A. From Tobago, one of the Caribbees; but very little, if any, now comes from it.

Q. Who first introduced the use of it into England?

A. Sir Walter Raleigh, in the reign of Elizabeth.

Q. When did smoking come into fashion?

A. In the reign of James the First, but it was not introduced at court, the king disliking the smell. He used to say *he had no notion of men making a chimney of their mouths.*

Q. What people smoke this plant and consider it a great luxury?

A. The Germans and Dutch, but it has of late years been much indulged in by the English and other nations.

Q. What is snuff?

A. Only tobacco ground to a very fine powder, and scented; but it is also made from the stalk of the tobacco plant.

Q. When was snuff introduced into France?

A. In the reign of Henry III.; it was called *l'herbe à la reine,* Catherine de Medicis being very fond of it.

Q. Where do the famous cigars called cheroots come from?

A. They are manufactured only at Manilla, the principal city of the Philippines. Seven thousand women are employed from morning till evening in this manufacture, which supplies the whole world with this fashionable luxury.

Q. What is rhubarb?

A. The root of a plant which grows wild in Turkey in Asia, and Arabia Felix; it is a very valuable medicine.

Q. Is it the same plant which is used for pies and tarts in the spring?

A. No; that species grows wild on the mountains of Rhodope in Thrace, and is now cultivated in kitchen-gardens for the sake of the stalks.

Q. When was this plant introduced into England?

A. About the year 1810, by Mr. Miatt, a gardener at Deptford.

Q. Was it not some time before the poorer classes could be induced to purchase it?

A. Yes; for they fancied that rhubarb must be a kind of physic.

Q. What is calomel?

A. A preparation from the metal quicksilver.

Q. Is not calomel a very fine and useful medicine?

A. Yes; in a variety of diseases it has been found most valuable.

Q. What is magnesia?

A. It is prepared by dissolving Epsom salts in water, and adding to the solution half their weight in potash.

Q. How does this produce magnesia?

A. The substance which sinks to the bottom, when washed well with water and dried, becomes a light, soft, and white powder, without taste, which is called magnesia: it is now chiefly procured from magnesian limestone.

Q. What are Epsom salts?

A. They are found in masses, on rocks and stones, or dissolved in mineral waters, as at Epsom in Surrey, and Seidlitz in Bohemia: it is also obtained from magnesian limestone; the taste is bitter and unpleasant.

Q. What is senna?

A. The dried leaves of an annual plant, brought from Alexandria, and from Ghezan in Arabia Felix, which are made up into a valuable medicinal tea.

Q. What is sarsaparilla?

A. The long fibrous root of a rough bind-weed plant, which flourishes in low moist ground and near the banks of rivers.

Q. Where is it much cultivated?

A. In Jamaica, for its medicinal properties in purifying the blood.

Q. What is peppermint?

A. A strong aromatic oil, distilled from a British plant which grows in watery places.

Q. Is not the well-known liquor called peppermint-water prepared from this plant?

A. Yes; and it is more used in medicine than any other distilled water.

Q. What is ipecacuanha?

A. The root of several plants growing in Brazil, New Granada, and other parts of South America; it is used in medicine.

Q. What is Peruvian bark?

A. The bark of a tree growing in Peru; it is called by the Spaniards fever-wood.

Q. Why?

A. Because of its extraordinary virtue in removing all kinds of fevers and agues.

Q. What do the Indians call this tree?

A. The fuddling-tree; because it is said to intoxicate all the fish in the water where the wood or bark has been steeped.

Q. What other name is it also known by?

A. That of Jesuit's bark, because it was first introduced into Europe by some persons of that religious order.

Q. What king was cured by it of a fever, when Dauphin of France?

A. Louis the Fourteenth.

Q. What is quinine?

A. A valuable preparation from Peruvian bark, lately discovered.

Q. What are aloes?

A. The juice of the Socotrine aloe, prepared from the leaves when fresh cut, which juice, when dried in the sun, becomes a hard substance.

Q. Is not this also a valuable medicine?

A. Yes; and this aloe grows in abundance in the island of Socotra, near the mouth of the Red Sea.

Q. What beautiful colour do the leaves of the Socotrine aloe afford?

A. A violet which does not require any mordant to fix it.

Q. By what people is the aloe dedicated to the offices of religion?

A. By the Mahometans and Egyptians; and pilgrims, on their return from Mecca, hang it over their doors, to show that they have performed that holy journey.

Q. What is the balm of Mecca?

A. A costly gum-resin, brought from Arabia and Turkey, of a very grateful taste and flavour, used in medicine.

Q. What is the balm of Gilead?

A. The dried juice of a low shrub growing in Abyssinia and Syria.

Q. Is it not very scarce and valuable?

A. Yes; for the quantity of balsam yielded by one tree never exceeds sixty drops a day.

Q. Was it not in great esteem in ancient times?

A. Yes; for Josephus informs us the balsam of Gilead was one of the

presents given by the Queen of Sheba
to King Solomon.

Q. What is it good for?

A. To strengthen the stomach and
excite the spirits.

Q. What is the balsam of Tolu?

A. It is obtained from a tree which
grows to a considerable height in the
province of Tolu, near the isthmus of
Panama in South America.

Q. How is it procured?

A. Incisions are made in the bark of
the trees, and a resinous fluid oozes out,
of a yellowish-white colour.

Q. Is not its smell very grateful?

A. Yes; it resembles that of lemons,
and its taste is warm and sweetish.

Q. How is this balsam used?

A. Both in the form of a tincture
and a syrup; it is also made into lo-
zenges for coughs.

Q. What is quassia?

A. A very bitter drug; the root of a
tree, so called from a slave of the name
of Quassi, who used it with great success in the malignant fevers which prevail in Surinam.

Q. What part of the tree is made use of in medicine?

A. The root, bark, and wood; it is a valuable drug in nervous diseases.

Q. What country is it a native of?

A. The colony of Surinam, and South America generally.

Q. What is assafœtida?

A. A valuable medicinal gum produced from a plant resembling the cauliflower.

Q. Where does it grow?

A. Most plentifully on mountains in the provinces of Chorassan, and Laar, in Persia.

Q. Is not the process of obtaining it very curious?

A. Yes; the top of the roots of the oldest plants must be cleared, and then the leaves and stalks are twisted together to screen it from the sun.

Q. How long does it remain in this state?

A. Forty days, when the top of the root is cut off, and it is again screened for forty-eight hours, when a fine juice

U

can be scraped off, which is exposed to
the sun to harden.

Q. How often is this operation performed on the same plant in order to
gain the juice?

A. Eight times, which occupies a period of six weeks; the juice has a most
nauseous smell and taste.

Q. What is goulard?

A. A preparation from the extract of
lead, of great use in allaying inflamma-
tions.

Q. What is benzoin?

A. A thick, whitish, resinous juice,
which oozes from a tree that grows
chiefly in the island of Sumatra.

Q. Does it not form the principal ingredient of what is called Friar's Balsam?

A. Yes; the properties of which, for
healing flesh cuts, are well known.

Q. Is it not also used in making
court-plaster?

A. Yes; isinglass is dissolved and laid
with a brush on thick black sarsenet,
which is afterwards washed over with a

weak solution of benzoin in spirits of wine.

Q. What countries use great quantities of gum-benzoin?

A. Those where the Roman Catholic and Mahometan religions prevail: it is burned as incense in their churches and mosques.

Q. What is storax?

A. A fragrant balsam, like benzoin, used in medicine, and burnt as a perfume.

Q. What is gum-guaiacum?

A. The resin of a large West Indian tree, every part of which is useful; the bark, resin, and flowers are used as medicine, and the wood is most valuable to the turner.

Q. What forms the famous diamond cement?

A. Isinglass dissolved in alcohol with gum-ammoniac; it is so named because the Turks employ it in setting their precious stones or jewelry: for if well made, the cement preserves its transparency after the setting.

Q. What is hartshorn?

A. It is now distilled from bones, but formerly it was only prepared from the horns of the deer or hart, and hence its name hartshorn.

Q. What are cantharides, or Spanish flies?

A. Insects about an inch in length, valuable as being used for blistering plasters.

Q. From whence are they brought?

A. We receive them in a dry state from Spain, Italy, the south of France, Sicily, and St. Petersburg.

Q. How are they collected?

A. Very easily: for during the day they are in a torpid state, and are shaken from the trees upon a cloth spread on the ground.

Q. How are they destroyed?

A. When a number have been collected they are tied in bags, and killed by being held over the steam of hot vinegar and then dried in the sun.

Q. Have they not a very powerful and nauseous smell?

A. Yes; and before being used for a blister they are pounded.

Q. What are leeches?

A. A worm-shaped animal found in muddy waters; in much use in medicine for drawing or sucking blood, which they do with three sharp little teeth.

Q. Where are they found?

A. In several of the rivers in the south of England; but they now come principally from Hungary and Poland, from whence they are sent to Hamburgh, where the Jews procure them for the London dealers at great expense.

Q. How are they caught?

A. In various ways; but one of the best is to throw bundles of weeds into the water where they are: these if taken out a few hours after, will have numbers found sticking to them.

Q. Are there not various species of leech?

A. Yes; the gray, commonly called the speckled, the green, and the black; the first two are the only ones used in surgery, the black, or horse leech being considered venomous.

Q. What is arsenic?

A. A most deadly poison, found abundantly in mines in Cornwall and Devonshire: a few grains will prove fatal; and it has often been mistaken for salt or white sugar.

Q. What is oxalic acid?

A. A very active poisonous juice, found plentifully in the well-known plant, called wood-sorrel. It is chiefly used by calico-printers and straw-bonnet makers.

Q. What is dragon's blood?

A. A red kind of resin forced out of the fruit of the rotang plant, when exposed by the Japanese over the steam of boiling water.

Q. Is it not a curious plant?

A. Yes; it is a species of cane, and grows to the length of a hundred feet, about as thick as a man's arm: it is chiefly used in red colouring, and sometimes in medicine.

Q. What is castor oil?

A. It is an oil obtained by pressing

the seed of a plant growing in both the East and West Indies; there are also large plantations of it in Nubia and the adjoining countries.

Q. Where is Nubia?

A. In Africa, to the south of Egypt.

Q. Is it not a valuable medicine?

A. Yes; the seeds are bruised in a mortar, afterwards tied in linen bags, and boiled in water, until the oil rises to the top, which is carefully skimmed off and bottled.

Q. Is not castor oil much used in Nubia?

A. Yes; the smooth, shining skin of the Nubians owes all its brilliancy to being frequently rubbed with castor oil.

Q. Why do they apply castor oil to their bodies?

A. To prevent them from being scorched by the rays of the tropical sun.

Q. What is mastic?

A. A fine gum brought from Scio, an island in the Archipelago, and from the Levant; the Turkish women chew it to make their teeth white, and burn it with other fine gums as a perfume.

Q. Which are the principal metals?

A. Gold, silver, platina, copper, iron, lead, and tin.

Q. Which are the most precious of all these metals?

A. Gold and silver.

Q. Which is the heaviest, hardest, and most difficult to be melted?

A. Platina.

Q. Which is the lightest?

A. Tin.

Q. Which is the most useful?

A. Iron.

Q. Why?

A. Because no instrument, machine, or scarcely any thing else can be made without the help of it.

Q. Where does gold come from?

A. It is found in most hot countries: New Mexico, and North America, the East Indies and Brazil.

Q. Has not a very abundant supply of gold been discovered of late years?

A. Yes; in California in the year

1847, and in Australia in the year 1851: it covers the face of a large portion of these countries.

Q. Where is California?

A. It is a peninsula on the western side of America : it has been recently added to the United States.

Q. Is gold easily obtained from California?

A. No ; the diggings, where the gold is found, frequently cannot be worked on account of the weather: and the diggers suffer many other privations.

Q. Is California easy of access ?

A. No ; for unless a person going from Europe to New York chooses to take a long and fatiguing overland journey, he must go round the south of South America, through the Straits of Magellan.

Q. Where is Australia?

A. An immense island south of China, about the size of Europe; it was formerly called New Holland.

Q. To whom does it belong ?

A. It is one of the most important

u 5

colonies of the British Empire, and has recently attracted much attention on account of the quantity of gold found there.

Q. Where are the three principal settlements ?

A. On the south-eastern side : they are called South Australia, Victoria, (formerly called Port Philip,) and New South Wales.

Q. How is gold found ?

A. Generally in a rock called quartz, and sometimes in lumps almost pure, called nuggets.

Q. Is it ever found in large masses ?

A. Yes, but seldom : in July, 1851, a piece of quartz was discovered, from which sixty lbs. weight of pure gold was obtained.

Q. Was not a new discovery of gold made in the year 1858 ?

A. Yes ; in a part of Canada which has been made into a province by the name of British Columbia ; it is situate on the west coast of North America, being bounded by the Pacific Ocean.

Q. Is not gold sometimes found in the sand and mud of rivers?

A. Yes; particularly in Guinea, in Africa: and much gold is also procured from the rivers Senegal, Gambia, and the Niger.

Q. Has not Africa always been famous for gold?

A. Yes; the ancients had much from it, particularly King Solomon; for the famous Ophir is thought to have been where the Sofala now stands; and Herodotus tells us, that the king of Ethiopia brought to Cambyses all his prisoners bound with chains of gold!

Q. What river is said to have been the chief source of the long famous riches of King Crœsus?

A. Pactōlus, a river in Lydia, said to have golden sands; it runs by Sardis, and empties itself into the Archipelago.

Q. From what countries is the greatest quantity of gold now obtained?

A. From California and Australia: but large quantities are brought from Brazil. The discovery of gold there was made by a party of soldiers sent to quell an insurrection, who found among the natives fish-hooks, &c., made of gold.

Q. Did not this lead to some inquiry?

A. Yes; and they were told the gold was brought down from the mountains by the floods, when the torrents came rushing into the valleys. This was enough to cause a diligent search, and the quantities of grains found after the floods exceeded belief.

Q. Which are the principal gold mines in Europe?

A. Those of Hungary and Saltzburg. Spain is also thought to be very rich in gold; but since the discovery of America the mines have not been worked. A considerable quantity of gold is brought from the Ural Mountains.

Q. Where are they?

A. At the north-eastern border of Europe, dividing that continent from Asia: they are in the dominions of the Emperor of Russia.

Q. Has the value of gold been long known?

A. Yes; from the earliest ages of the world: it is used for coinage, and is employed principally in jewelry and gilding.

Q. What is silver?

A. A white brilliant metal chiefly found in the mines at Potosi, in South America: there are several good mines in Norway and Sweden, but they are not worked now. Much silver is extracted from lead ore.

Q. Who discovered the famous silver mine at Potosi?

A. An Indian called Hualpa: he discovered it by chance. In scampering after a wild animal, he laid hold of the branch of a shrub, which his weight tore up by the roots, and to his surprise he found several small bits of silver sticking to it.

Q. Did he reap much benefit from his luck?

A. No; he made a confidant of a friend who betrayed the secret to the

Spaniards, who soon took possession of it in 1545.

Q. Is not Peru very rich in mines of gold and silver?

A. Yes; it is said to contain sixty-nine mines of gold, and seven hundred and eighty-four of silver.

Q. Is not silver the most precious of all metals next to gold?

A. Yes; except, perhaps, platina; and it is also, like gold, coined into money, and manufactured into various utensils, such as goblets, vases, forks, spoons, and dishes.

Q. What renders both gold and silver so very valuable and useful?

A. Their ductility, or capability of being drawn out without breaking into a wire much finer than a human hair, or beaten into leaves so fine, that they will hardly bear breathing upon.

Q. When beaten so delicately fine, what is gold used for?

A. Gilding.

Q. Was not the gold thread used by the Egyptians and Israelites in their fine embroidery the solid metal beaten out exquisitely fine, and then rounded ?

A. Yes; and continued to be used so till about the time of the Emperor Aurelian, when a silken thread with a gold coating was substituted, and has ever since continued.

Q. Were not the Jewish maidens beholden to their residence in Egypt for the perfection they attained in the art of embroidery ?

A. Yes; which they afterwards displayed so worthily in the service of the tabernacle, as described in the Bible.

Q. What is platina ?

A. A white metal, not so bright as silver, found formerly only in small grains or scales, in the sands of some of the rivers of South America, but now also in the Ural Mountains.

Q. If it could be obtained in sufficient quantities, would it not be very valuable and useful ?

A. Yes; for its ductility is as great if not greater than that of gold or silver: and, like them, it will not rust.

Q. Which are the perfect metals ?

A. Gold, silver, and platina.

Q. Why are these called perfect ?

A. Because they lose nothing in weight or value by the heat of the fire.

Q. Does this not mean that they are not destroyed or wasted by being melted in the fire?

A. Yes.

Q. Is this the case with other metals ?

A. No ; they are all changed by fire into a powdered kind of matter called calx.

Q. Are not these, then, called the imperfect metals ?

A. Yes ; for they lose by the heat of the fire, and can easily be dissolved or corroded by acids.

Q. What do you mean by the word corrode ?

A. To rust or eat away by degrees.

Q. What is an acid ?

A. Any thing sour or sharp.

Q. What is iron ?

A. A well-known metal ; its value and uses were familiar to the people in the time of Moses, who tells us of swords, knives, &c., which were made in his time.

Q. Where is iron found ?

A. The finest iron mines at present are those in Great Britain.

Q. But is it not found in most of the countries of Europe?

A. Yes; as well as in almost every country in the world.

Q. Where are the best iron mines in England?

A. Colebrook Dale, in Shropshire, and the Forest of Dean, in Gloucester-shire; but the largest quantities are obtained from Lanarkshire and Glamor-ganshire.

Q. Are not the mines in Dean Forest ancient?

A. Yes; they were worked by the Romans.

Q. Is not the production of iron in Great Britain very immense ?

A. Yes; about four million tons annually; it has rapidly increased of late years.

Q. How many sorts of iron are there?

A. Three; forged or wrought iron, cast iron, and steel.

Q. What do you mean by forging iron?

A. Beating it out with large hammers when red hot.

Q. What effect has this on the iron?

A. It becomes softer and more flexible, and is easily bent.

Q. What is cast iron?

A. It is iron melted to a liquid in very hot furnaces.

Q. But how is it cast into pipes, pots, grates, and the numerous other forms we see it in?

A. By shapes being made of a kind of loam, or earthy substance, of the various forms wanted, and the melted liquid flowing from the furnace into them.

Q. When cold I suppose these moulds are removed?

A. Yes; and the iron is in the shape wanted.

Q. Are cannons now cast in this way?

A. No; it was found not to insure the great strength required: they are first cast solid, after which the centre is bored out by a machine.

Q. What is the difference between wrought iron and cast iron?

A. Wrought iron is only heated and beaten into shapes; cast iron is melted and run into moulds.

Q. What Emperor learnt the trade of a blacksmith, in order to set an example to his subjects?

A. Peter the Great, the Czar or Emperor of Russia, in the reign of our William and Mary.

Q. At what place did he perform his laborious work?

A. At Istia, a place not far from Moscow, where he once passed a month: and also at Olonetz, situate on the side of Lake Ladoga.

Q. When he worked at the forge, what did he make the boyards or noblemen do?

A. He obliged them to blow the bellows, stir the fire, carry coals, and perform all the other offices of blacksmiths.

Q. What king worked as a common labourer in the iron mines of Dalecarlia, in Sweden?

A. Gustavus Vasa. The miners enabled him to resist the tyrannical Danish king, Christian the Second; his memory is still held in great veneration.

Q. Is not iron of far more real value than gold?

A. Yes; for without it the earth could not have been cultivated, nor houses, cities, and ships built; and few arts could have been practised.

Q. Has not this country been immensely benefited by the discovery of the power of steam?

A. Yes; we owe this great discovery to James Watt, a native of Scotland, who first turned it to account in the year 1769, but he subsequently made many great improvements.

Q. When were vessels first propelled by steam in Great Britain?

A. In the year 1812, on the Clyde.

Q. What other great men ought we to remember when speaking of the immense benefits conferred on this country by James Watt?

A. George Stephenson, who first applied steam to propel locomotive engines on our railways.

Q. Are not the rails on railways made of iron?

A. Yes.

Q. Which was the first railway in England?

A. That from Liverpool to Manchester; it was opened September 15, 1830.

Q. Is not the Britannia Tubular Bridge across the Menai Straits from Carnarvonshire to the Isle of Anglesea very wonderful?

A. Yes; it is composed of two immense iron tubes, through which the railway trains pass, a hundred feet above the sea; each tube weighs about five thousand tons. They were suspended by means of hydraulic presses.

Q. But was the whole of each tube raised at one time?

A. No; it was composed of several portions, the largest of which is 472 feet long, 27 feet high, and weighs upwards of 1700 tons, and was elevated at once.

Q. Who constructed this wonderful bridge?

A. Our late great engineer, Mr. Robert Stephenson; it was opened in 1850.

Q. What do you mean by a hydraulic press?

A. A machine of enormous power arising from the pressure of water.

Q. But has not the Britannia Bridge now been surpassed?

A. Yes; by the Victoria Bridge which has been constructed as part of the Grand Trunk Railway of Canada, and was opened in 1859: this is the greatest work of the kind in the world.

Q. What is the object of this bridge?

A. It crosses the river St. Lawrence near Montreal, and is nearly *two miles* in length; the iron tubes weigh nearly 10,000 tons and they are supported by massive piers of solid masonry.

Q. Has not an iron ship been recently built in this country which may be called a wonder of the world?

A. Yes; the Great Eastern, which was launched at Millwall, on the Thames, in 1858.

Q. Can you tell me some of her dimensions?

A. Her length is 690 feet, and breadth 58 feet; she is of the burden of upwards of 22,000 tons, and constructed to carry 4000 passengers.

Q. Is this vessel much larger than a line of battle ship?

A. Yes; her tonnage is nearly four times that of the largest man-of-war in our navy.

Q. Has not iron been introduced recently in the construction of vessels for the navy?

A. Yes; some of our finest ships of war are made of wood overlaid with very thick plates of iron, or of solid iron.

Q. Does not this offer considerable resistance to the formidable artillery invented by Sir William Armstrong?

A. Yes.

Q. What is steel?

A. It is only a more perfect kind of iron formed by heating bars of iron with charcoal ashes covered with a kind of clay.

Q. For what purpose is this done?

A. To render it whiter, and of a much finer and closer grain, after which it will bear a very high polish.

Q. How does steel acquire its extreme hardness and brittleness?

A. By being plunged when hot into cold water; but if it be suffered to cool slowly it becomes soft.

Q. Where is the iron which is converted into steel chiefly found?

A. In Sweden, whence it is imported into this country.

Q. What does the hardness of steel render it capable of?

A. Receiving a very sharp edge, which makes it particularly useful for the blades of all instruments for cutting, such as swords, knives, razors, and scissors.

Q. Does not a pair of scissors occupy more time in making than any other article of cutlery?

A. Yes; because they are made by hand, and each pair passes through sixteen or seventeen hands, including fifty or sixty kinds of work, before it is ready for sale.

Q. Are not snuffers made in a similar way?

A. Yes.

Q. Are not razors made of the finest steel?

A. Yes; each razor passes through a dozen hands; it is ground and polished upon wheels, so as to make the blade hollow and give it a very fine edge.

Q. What is emery?

A. A hard, heavy iron ore, found in large masses, mixed with other minerals; the best comes from the Levant, and the Isle of Naxos in the Archipelago.

Q. How is it prepared?

A. It is ground in mills into a very fine powder, and is used by lapidaries in the cutting and polishing of precious stones.

Q. Is it only useful to lapidaries?

A. No; it is used in smoothing the

X

surface of the finer kinds of glass; by cutlers, in polishing iron and steel instruments; by masons, in the polishing of marble; and by numerous other artisans.

Q. Is not the loadstone, or leading stone, a kind of iron?

A. Yes; it is a rich iron ore, found in iron mines, in Germany, England, Arabia, and Bengal.

Q. What are its properties?

A. It attracts iron, giving it an inclination towards the north, and even causes a needle touched with it to point towards the poles of the earth.

Q. Has it any other property?

A. Yes; every magnet has two poles, one always pointing towards the north, and the other towards the south: this circumstance has rendered it of the greatest use in navigation.

Q. Does the needle point exactly to the true north and south?

A. No; it is called the magnetic north and south, and points about twenty degrees to the west of the true north.

Q. What is navigation?

A. The art of directing any vessel by water from one place to another.

Q. Has the discovery of the magnet enabled sailors to venture into the great ocean far away from any land?

A. Yes; by means of the mariner's compass they can find their way with as much ease in the midst of the ocean as they formerly did when they never lost sight of land.

Q. What is the mariner's compass?

A. The valuable needle or magnet, which always turns to the magnetic north; it is usually fixed in a round brass box, which contains a paper card, on which are marked the thirty-two points of the compass.

Q. Has any one ever discovered the cause of this extraordinary property?

A. No.

Q. What is copper?

A. A red-coloured metal, and the most sonorous of all metals.

Q. Where is it found?

A. By far the largest quantity now

comes from Cornwall; a considerable quantity is also found in Australia and the Isle of Anglesea.

Q. What is probably the most productive copper mine in the world?

A. The Burra Burra mine in South Australia, which contains a vein of copper seventeen feet thick.

Q. But is not copper found in every part of the world?

A. Yes.

Q. How many kinds of copper are there?

A. Three; the common, the rose copper, and the virgin copper.

Q. Do all these three kinds come from the same mine?

A. Yes; the difference between them is in the preparation.

Q. Is not copper sometimes mixed with other metals?

A. Yes; it forms several compound or mixed metals.

Q. What is bell-metal?

A. Copper mixed with a large quantity of tin; it is so called from bells being made of it, and is very hard and sonorous.

Q. When were bells first used for ecclesiastical purposes ?

A. About the sixth century : but they were not brought to any perfection until the time of Charlemagne.

Q. What bell is occasionally heard in London ?

A. The great bell of St. Paul's, which is tolled on the death of any member of the royal family.

Q. Which is the largest bell ever founded ?

A. The great bell at Moscow in the Kremlin. It is sixty-seven feet four inches in circumference, and was kept in a deep pit, where it was originally cast, and weighs 443,772 lbs.

Q. Was it ever moved ?

A. Not until 1837, when the Emperor Nicholas had it placed on a low circular wall. It is visited as one of the wonders of Moscow, which is celebrated for its bells.

Q. What other people are particularly fond of bells ?

A. The Chinese; at Pekin there are seven bells, each weighing 120,000 lbs., but the sound of them is poor, as they are struck with a wooden and not an iron clapper.

Q. What other noted bells are often spoken of?

A. The great bell at St. Peter's at Rome, weighing upwards of 18,000 lbs.; one at Florence, 17,000 lbs.; Great Tom of Christ Church, Oxford, 17,000 lbs.; Great Tom at Lincoln, 9894 lbs.; and St. Paul's, London, 8400 lbs.

Q. Have house bells been long used in England?

A. No; even in the reign of Queen Anne most of the old mansions of our nobility were without them.

Q. Was not this found inconvenient?

A. No; for some of the domestics were always in immediate attendance.

Q. Were not the ancients acquainted with the use of bells?

A. Yes; for many small bronze bells have been found in the excavations recently made at Nineveh.

Q. Was not the site of this famous city unknown for more than 2000 years?

A. Yes; until discovered a few years since in the neighbourhood of Mosul, in Mesopotamia, by our enterprising countryman, Mr. Layard, who has published several interesting works upon the subject.

Q. Are not many of the sculptures and relics mentioned by Mr. Layard to be seen in this country?

A. Yes; at the British Museum, in London.

Q. What is bronze?

A. Copper mixed with a less quantity of tin; this composition must have been known in very early times.

Q. Why?

A. Because it is mentioned in the Old Testament; and we learn also from Homer, that in the Trojan war, the combatants had no other armour than what was made of bronze.

Q. Is not this a little doubtful?

A. Perhaps so, as the Greek word

" kalkos " frequently signifies brass, and it is very likely that the word, as used by them, meant iron as well as brass.

Q. What is pinchbeck, or prince's metal?

A. Copper mixed with zinc; it is of nearly the same colour as gold, and is used for common watch-cases, &c.

Q. How came it to be called prince's metal?

A. It was named after its inventor, Prince Rupert, an ingenious philosopher and gallant soldier, the nephew of Charles I.

Q. What is zinc?

A. A metal of a brilliant white colour, with a shade of blue, extremely useful and valuable, as it mixes well with most other metals.

Q. What is verdigris?

A. It is that green substance so often seen on dirty copper, and may be called its rust.

Q. Is it not a rank poison?

A. Yes: and this renders copper

vessels very dangerous, unless kept perfectly clean.

Q. Where is there a large manufactory of verdigris?

A. At Montpellier, in the south of France : the husks of grapes are placed between copper plates, and the acid soon collects the rust.

Q. What is then done with it?

A. It is scraped off as it collects; afterwards dried, and put in bags or casks for sale.

Q. For what is it principally used?

A. For dyeing a fine black, when mixed with logwood; also for giving a beautiful green to porcelain, and for green paint, &c.

Q. Is not copper of great use in covering or sheathing the bottoms of ships?

A. Yes; it preserves them from worms, and its smoothness is said to promote the swiftness of their sailing.

Q. What sort of a metal is lead?

A. It is a coarse, soft, impure metal, but a very useful one.

Q. Whence have we lead?

A. Great Britain possesses the most important lead mines in the world; the best known are in Flintshire, Derbyshire, Cornwall, Devonshire, Northumberland, and Durham.

Q. For what purpose is it generally used?

A. Houses and churches are sometimes covered with lead: gutters, pipes, and cisterns are also made of it.

Q. Is not this metal of a very poisonous quality?

A. Yes; so much so, that in the neighbourhood where it is dug, neither dog, cat, nor fowl can be kept.

Q. What is white lead?

A. It is made by holding thin plates of lead over heated vinegar.

Q. What does this process cause?

A. The acid rising from the vinegar corrodes the lead and converts it into a heavy white powder.

Q. By whom is white lead used?

A. By house painters, who mix it with oil to thicken their paints.

Q. Is not white lead very prejudicial to health?

A. Yes; being a slow poison.

Q. Is there any other useful preparation of lead?

A. Yes; red lead, or minium, also used as a colour by painters: it is used in the manufacture of glass and for other purposes.

Q. What is tin?

A. A metal of a whitish colour.

Q. What country has long been noted for producing it?

A. Cornwall; so long ago as 700 years before the birth of Christ the Phœnicians traded to this country for that article.

Q. Who were the Phœnicians?

A. The inhabitants of the celebrated country of Phœnicia, in Asia, now called Syria: Tyre and Sidon were the capital towns of this country.

Q. What celebrated queen left her wicked brother Pygmalion, king of Tyre, and founded the renowned city of Carthage?

A. Queen Dido.

Q. Are the uses of tin very considerable?

A. Yes; its freedom from rust renders
it very valuable for all vessels used for
cooking.

Q. What is block-tin?

A. It is tin melted in a furnace, and
poured into moulds of stone containing
320 pounds' weight, which are stamped
with the impression of a lion, the arms
of the duchy of Cornwall.

Q. What duty does it pay?

A. Four shillings per hundredweight.

Q. Who receives this fine revenue?

A. The Prince of Wales, the eldest
son of the sovereign of England, as
Duke of Cornwall, which is one of his
titles.

Q. What is solder?

A. A strong cement, formed by melting lead and tin into a liquid, used
for joining the different parts of metals
together.

Q. What is pewter?

A. A composition made of lead and tin.

Q. What is its use?

A. It was formerly much used for dishes and plates; but earthenware, which is much cleaner and pleasanter, has almost rendered it useless, except for the pots of the publicans.

Q. What is brass?

A. A compound metal made of copper mixed with zinc, or the calamine stone, which renders it yellow and hard.

Q. What is calamine stone?

A. A stone found plentifully in England, the Netherlands, and Germany.

Q. How is it procured?

A. It is dug out of the ground, roasted five or six hours, passed through a sieve, ground in a mill, and in this state is sold.

Q. Where is the great demand for it?

A. At Birmingham, for the brass foundries in that town.

Q. Where is the finest brass manufactured?

A. At Geneva, a fortified town in a canton of the same name in Switzerland.

Y

Q. What is quicksilver, or mercury?

A. An imperfect metal, resembling melted silver, of great use in manufactures and medicine : it is the heaviest of all fluids.

Q. Where is it found?

A. In Germany, Hungary, Italy, Spain, and South America.

Q. What is the great use of quicksilver?

A. That of extracting other metals from their ores, particularly gold and silver, for without the aid of this mineral it would not be easy to clear those more precious metals; it was used upwards of 1000 years B.C. for the same purpose.

Q. Is there not a famous mine of quicksilver in Peru?

A. Yes, at Guanza Velica; it has been worked almost 300 years, and is quite a subterraneous city, with broad streets, open squares, and a chapel. Thousands of flambeaux are kept continually burning.

Q. Where are there two other noted mines?

A. At Idria, a town of Austria, in Carniola; it belongs to the Emperor of Austria: and the other is near the town of Almaden, in the province of La Mancha in Spain.

Q. Is it not a most noxious mineral to procure?

A. Yes; the miners suffer dreadfully from languors and convulsions; the most robust constitutions seldom last above a couple of years; consequently persons condemned for certain crimes are sent to labour in these fatal mines.

Q. What does mercury form, combined with tin?

A. The silvering of looking-glasses.

Q. What is vitriol?

A. A mineral salt: there are three sorts of vitriol, green, blue, and white.

Q. How is green vitriol formed?

A. By a combination of iron and sulphuric acid; it is used in making writing-ink, Prussian blue, and for other purposes.

Q. How is blue vitriol formed?

A. By a combination of copper and

sulphuric acid; it is used by artists and manufacturers, and is employed in dyeing.

Q. Is not the beautiful grass-green colour of the chemists' shops made from blue vitriol?

A. Yes; and fowling-pieces and tea-urns are browned by washing them with a preparation of vitriol.

Q. What is white vitriol?

A. It is composed of sulphuric acid and zinc.

Q. What is it used in?

A. Medicine; and varnishers and dyers use great quantities of it to render deeper the colours produced by madder, cochineal, &c.

Q. What is borax?

A. A salt of a brownish grey colour and a sweetish taste, brought from Thibet, and the East Indies: it is also found in South America and Italy.

Q. Was not the art of refining it kept for a long time a secret by the Dutch and Venetians?

A. Yes. Its uses are numerous; it

is employed in making the finest glass, and jewellers use it for the better soldering of gold and silver : it is also used in medicine.

Q. Has not a recent discovery been made, the result of which will make borax more plentiful ?

A. Yes ; within the last few years hot vapours arising from the earth have been discovered in Tuscany, from which large quantities of borax are obtained ; these vapours are called borax lagoons.

Q. What is potash ?

A. It is a salt or alkali, found in vegetable substances, obtained by burning them.

Q. Why is it called potash ?

A. From its having formerly been prepared in large iron pots.

Q. For what purpose is it used ?

A. In many arts and manufactures ; in scouring, washing, bleaching, dyeing, glass-making, &c.

Q. What is pearlash ?

A. It is only potash burnt red-hot, which renders it whiter and more pure.

Q. What is fullers' earth?

A. A well-known clay, of a greenish yellow colour, very valuable for its property of taking grease out of woollen and other cloths.

Q. What country is famous for it?

A. England: and this enables us to bring our broad cloths to such perfection, as no other country produces fullers' earth equal to ours.

Q. Might it not be used in most instances as a substitute for soap?

A. Yes.

Q. What is pipe-clay?

A. It is a fine common clay; tobacco-pipes are made of it, by casting them in moulds; and it is used for many domestic purposes.

Q. Is it not the principal ingredient of the common yellow, or kitchen ware?

A. Yes.

Q. What is soda?

A. It is a salt or alkali, like potash, obtained from sea-water, and different kinds of plants that grow on the sea-shores, but chiefly now from common salt.

Q. Is it not sometimes called barilla?

A. Yes; this is the Spanish name for it; it is principally used in making glass and soap.

Q. What is soap?

A. It is made of soda, tallow, or oil, mixed with other things, and is prepared by boiling.

Q. What is soft soap?

A. It is made like other soap, except that potash is used instead of soda.

Q. What is phosphorus?

A. A combustible substance, like bees' wax in colour and consistence; it is not known in a natural state, but is made by different artificial processes.

Q. Is it not bright and shining in the dark, when exposed to the air?

A. Yes; and when melted should be kept under water, for fear of its catching fire.

Q. What is the greater part of the phosphorus sold in the shops obtained from?

A. Bones.

Q. What does combustible mean?

A. That which easily takes fire.

Q. What is asbestos?

A. It is a silvery white mineral, of silky, long, slender filaments, which is found in mountainous countries abroad, and in Anglesea, and Scotland.

Q. What is its name derived from?

A. "Asbestos," a Greek word which signifies *inconsumable*, or not capable of being burnt.

Q. What was it called by the ancients?

A. Amiantus; they made it into a kind of cloth, in which they burned the bodies of their dead, and thus they were enabled to collect the ashes without mixture.

Q. How is this curious cloth cleaned when greased or dirty?

A. By throwing it into a clear bright fire, the stains will burn out, and the cloth become of a dazzling whiteness.

Q. Did not the Romans purchase this cloth at an enormous expense?

A. Yes; and Pliny tells us he had seen table-cloths, towels, and napkins made of it.

Q. What is it now used for?

A. Chiefly small articles, by way of curiosity; such as caps, gloves, purses, girdles, &c.

Q. What is pumice-stone?

A. A light porous mineral, chiefly brought from the neighbourhood of volcanoes.

Q. What is it used for?

A. It is employed for smoothing the surface of wood, leather, metal, stones, glass, and other substances, and consequently is an article of considerable trade.

Q. From what places is it exported in great quantities?

A. From the Lipari Islands, to the north of the island of Sicily; they are all of volcanic origin.

Q. What is marble?

A. A kind of stone dug out of pits, or quarries, very hard, compact, and firm; capable of being most highly polished.

Q. Are there not various kinds of marble?

A. Yes; some are white or black, others variegated with stains, clouds, waves, and veins, but all opaque.

Q. What is the meaning of opaque?

A. Not transparent, dark.

Q. What countries in Europe are famous for their fine marbles?

A. Greece, Italy, Spain, France, and Great Britain; the black and the pure brilliant white marbles, which come from Carrara, are most highly valued.

Q. Where is Carrara?

A. A town in the duchy of Massa in Italy.

Q. Is not the Parian marble thought to be the purest and most lasting?

A. Yes; and it is in consequence used for the finest statues in marble.

Q. From whence is it procured?

A. From Paros, an island in the Archipelago: Phidias and Praxiteles, two celebrated ancient statuaries, were natives of it.

Q. What fine Grecian statue made of Parian marble is still an object of wonder and delight?

A. The Medicean Venus.

Q. What English counties produce very beautiful marble?

A. Derbyshire, Devonshire, and West-moreland; the Isle of Sky, and Suther-land, in Scotland; and numerous other places.

Q. What is verde-antique?

A. A beautiful green marble, found only in Egypt: if it ever came from Italy, the quarries are not now known.

Q. What is porphyry?

A. It is a beautiful stone, found in quarries, or beds of considerable magnitude.

Q. Where?

A. The principal quarries of porphyry are in Egypt: it is also found in various parts of Europe.

Q. Are there not many beautiful and splendid works in porphyry?

A. Yes; obelisks, statues, and columns are frequently made of it; it can be polished as highly as marble, but it is so hard that the expense of working it has caused it to be much neglected.

Q. What is alabaster?

A. It is a species of limestone found in masses, hanging like immense icicles from the roofs of caverns.

Q. Where is it found?

A. In most caverns in every country: those of Derbyshire are well known.

Q. Which is the most celebrated cave of this kind?

A. That of Antiparos, in the Grecian Archipelago.

Q. What is it used for?

A. To cut into vases, statues, tables, boxes, and other beautiful ornamental things.

Q. But is there not another kind of alabaster called gypsum, which is made into chimney-pieces, columns, busts, vases, lamps, &c.?

A. Yes; this gypsum is found in Cheshire, Derbyshire, and in many parts of the Continent; but that which is brought from Italy and Spain is the best.

Q. Was it not used by the ancients for windows?

A. Yes; as it admitted a soft and pleasing light without being transparent.

Q. To what uses did the ancients apply vases?

A. To hold the incense in their sacrifices, and after burning the dead bodies of their relations, they deposited their ashes in a vase or urn.

Q. Who copied many of these truly beautiful and elegant vessels?

A. Wedgwood : the British Museum affords a fine display of some of them.

Q. What is plaster of Paris?

A. It is alabaster heated till it falls into a soft white powder, which, when mixed with water, forms a paste called plaster of Paris.

Q. What is it employed for?

A. In the making of casts, statues, &c.: it is of a beautiful white colour, but very brittle.

Q. What is jasper?

A. A variegated, very hard stone, with stripes and shades of yellow, red, green, and white, with black dots.

Q. What is it principally used for?

A. It is made into vases, snuff-boxes, and other ornaments, as it will bear a very high polish; also for pillars in very grand buildings.

Q. What country has very fine quarries of it?

A. Spain.

Q. Where is it found?

A. In every quarter of the world; Egyptian jasper is found near Suez, in Egypt; Siberia produces a most beautiful kind for ornaments; and Tokay in Hungary, and Constantinople produce it.

Q. Where is there a splendid shrine of jasper?

A. In the cathedral church of Cologne; it is said to contain the remains of the three magi, or wise men, who went to Bethlehem to worship the Messiah.

Q. What are they generally called?

A. The three kings of Cologne. The shrine is adorned with a profusion of pearls and precious stones; the wise men are seen in full length, each having on his head a crown richly garnished with jewels.

Q. What is malachite?

A. A beautiful green copper ore, very

like green jasper, capable of being cut and polished as a gem, and made into trinkets; but it is principally used for slabs and tops of tables.

Q. Where are the best specimens found?

A. In Russia; in the Russian department at the Great Exhibition of 1851 there were some very magnificent vases, doors, and other large articles made of this beautiful composition.

Q. What is lapis lazuli?

A. A stone of a beautiful dark colour with dots, which look like golden veins or spots.

Q. Where is it chiefly found?

A. In Persia, Natolia, and China, Siberia, and Tartary; in Europe it has only been discovered in Germany, and among the ruins of Rome.

Q. What is jet?

A. A black opaque mineral, found in detached masses in several countries of the Continent; it is often cast on the shores of England, in Norfolk and Yorkshire.

Q. What is it valuable for?

A. Trinkets, such as ear-rings, necklaces, &c.; and in Roman Catholic countries great quantities are used for rosaries and crosses.

Q. What is agate?

A. The name of agate is derived from the river Achates, in Sicily, near which these stones were found in abundance by the ancients.

Q. Where are they now found?

A. In Scotland, Saxony, and Hungary; and they are also brought from China and the East Indies.

Q. What are they used for?

A. In jewelry for seals, &c.; also for magnificent cups, handles for splendid knives and forks, hilts for swords, and the tops of snuff-boxes.

Q. What are petrifactions?

A. Substances immersed in water strongly impregnated with lime, which has the power of covering any thing laid in it with a strong stony coat.

Q. What well in England is celebrated for these curiosities?

A. The dropping well at Knaresborough in Yorkshire.

Q. Is there not a curious specimen in the British Museum?

A. Yes; it is a human skull completely encrusted with stone, which was found in the river Tiber.

Q. What is coal?

A. Till lately considered a black *mineral*, principally obtained from the neighbourhood of Newcastle-upon-Tyne, Sunderland, and Whitehaven.

Q. What is now the opinion?

A. That coals are fossils, produced from forests which have been overwhelmed by the earth.

Q. But is not coal abundant in many other parts of Great Britain?

A. Yes; principally in Wales, Yorkshire, Derbyshire, Staffordshire, and the county of Lanark in Scotland. By means of the railway, these inland coals are now conveyed to most parts of the kingdom.

Q. Was not the burning of coal in the time of Whittington considered such a nuisance, that it was prohibited under a severe penalty?

A. Yes; but by the time he had been three times Lord Mayor, about 1419, the importation of coal had become a considerable branch of commerce.

Q. Do not foreigners imagine that our great wealth arises from the abundance of coals we possess?

A. Yes; as they afford the great means of carrying on all our valuable manufactures.

Q. When were coals generally adopted as fuel?

A. Not until the beginning of the reign of Charles I., though they are mentioned in the reign of Henry III.

Q. How long is it calculated that Newcastle and its neighbourhood can supply us with coal?

A. For many centuries, although the coal dug there and in other parts of the kingdom exceeds thirty millions of tons annually.

Q. What quantity of coal is annually brought into London alone?

A. Nearly four millions of tons.

Q. Are not the miners who work in the collieries subject to dreadful accidents?

A. Yes; the greatest danger arises from the foul air of the pit mixing with the common air, as then, upon approach of a lighted candle, or any other flame, it explodes like gunpowder.

Q. What did the late Sir Humphry Davy invent to prevent the loss of many valuable lives?

A. The safety-lamp, which is formed of such fine wire, that whilst it gives light, it will not allow the gas to explode: it was invented in 1816.

Q. What is gas?

A. A sort of inflammable air, found in many substances, but most plentifully in coal.

Q. Does it not produce a very brilliant light?

A. Yes, upon a candle or light being applied to it: and it is now in consequence generally used in our lamps instead of oil.

Q. How do they convey it?

A. By laying iron pipes from the reservoirs in which it is made, along the streets, underground, and from these large pipes small ones convey the gas into lamp-posts and houses.

Q. What is the light called *bude* light?

A. A very brilliant flame obtained by introducing a current of fresh air into a common gas light.

Q. What is cannel coal?

A. It is a peculiar coal, which gives a brilliant light like a candle, found in the neighbourhood of Wigan, in Lancashire.

Q. Does not this coal afford the best gas?

A. Yes.

Q. Will it not bear a high polish?

A. Yes; and it is so hard that it can be turned in a lathe, to form boxes and other ornamental articles.

Q. Is it not said that the black squares in the chequered pavement of Lichfield Cathedral are formed of cannel coal?

A. Yes; and the white ones are of alabaster.

Q. What is ether?

A. A very combustible fluid, produced by the action of acids upon spirits of wine.

Q. What is naphtha?

A. A yellowish kind of oil, of strong odour, issuing in springs from the ground. It is very inflammable.

Q. Is it of much use?

A. Yes; in dissolving various substances, as caoutchouc, india-rubber, &c.

Q. What is gamboge?

A. A vegetable gummy juice of a most beautiful yellow colour, chiefly brought from Cambodia, in the East Indies.

Q. What is its principal use?

A. It is much used in medicine, but its great value is in painting.

Q. What is vermilion?

A. A valuable red colour, formed of mercury and sulphur melted together and heated to redness.

Q. What is ultramarine?

A. The brilliant blue colour much esteemed by painters, and which we see so much used in the draperies of fine, splendid pictures.

Q. What is it made from?

A. Lapis lazuli; small pieces of which are chosen containing the most of this brilliant blue, which is burned or calcined to a fine powder, and made into a paste, with wax, linseed oil, &c.

Q. Is this all the preparation?

A. No; it is afterwards separated from these substances by washing, and the powder is prepared with great trouble and attention.

Q. Does it not last fresher and better than any other colour?

A. Yes; for that sweet colour is often seen quite bright, when all the rest in a picture are faded.

Q. What is cobalt?

A. A metal from which a beautiful blue is obtained, almost equal to ultramarine; it is found chiefly in the mines of Saxony, but also in those of Cornwall.

Q. What is umber?

A. A paint of a brown colour, compounded from a kind of iron ore, found in beds in the island of Cyprus.

Q. What is ochre?

A. A kind of earth or clay of various colours, as red, blue, yellow, brown, and green, in much use in oil and water painting, colouring washes, &c.

Q. What is annato?

A. A yellow dye prepared from a shrub called achrote, which grows in the West Indies. It is used in dyeing nankeen, and sometimes for colouring butter and cheese.

Q. What is fustic?

A. A yellow wood which grows in all the Caribbee Islands, used in dyeing yellow.

Q. What is sumach?

A. A yellow dye extracted from the leaves of a bushy tree of the same name growing in Spain, Portugal, Sicily, and Palestine.

Q. What is black chalk?

A. It is a soft earthy substance, valuable to crayon painters and other artists.

Q. Where is it found?

A. Great quantities are brought from France, Spain, and Italy; the best comes from the latter country.

Q. How is it prepared?

A. It is made into pencils, and they should be kept in a moist place.

Q. What is shagreen?

A. A kind of grained leather, prepared from the hides of asses and horses; but the proper shagreen is made from the skin of the shark or spotted dog-fish.

Q. What place is famous for the first of these manufactures?

A. Astrakan, a city of Tartary on the river Volga, of great trade and importance to the Russians.

Q. But from what place do we get the real shagreen?

A. The best comes from Constantinople; but we have it from the Persian Gulf, and from Tripoli and Algiers in Africa.

Q. What renders it valuable?

A. It makes a strong covering for cases, books, &c.

Q. Is not the skin of the ass useful for many other things?

A. Yes; on account of its hardness and elasticity it is made into heads of drums, leaves for pocket-books, &c. The ass is much valued in Spain.

Q. What are the most useful trees for cultivation?

A. The oak, elm, ash, beech, poplar, walnut, sweet chestnut, and fir.

Q. What is the oak useful for?

A. Every part of this noble tree has its use; the trunk is sawn into planks, to build ships and houses.

Q. How many oaks does it appear, from a printed Report made to the House of Commons, are required to build a 74-gun ship?

A. Two thousand trees of 75 years' growth: it requires 50 acres of ground to produce them, and they yield about 3000 loads of timber.

Q. How was the value of a man-of-war estimated?

A. By her guns: they reckoned she cost 1000*l.* a gun building, without her rigging; but the iron-clad vessels now used in the navy cost much more.

Q. When are oaks in the highest perfection for timber?

A. From 75 to 100, or at most 150 years old; the first age is that in which oak-trees are usually cut down for ship-building.

Q. Why is oak particularly used for ship-building?

A. Because no other wood is so durable in water.

Q. When the Spaniards sent out their Invincible Armada, what forest in England were the invaders ordered to destroy?

A. The Forest of Dean, in Gloucestershire, because the best oak for our shipping grew there; but Elizabeth's brave admirals and sailors prevented their having the opportunity.

Q. Has it not been lately proved that there are two distinct species of oak in England?

A. Yes; the native "Heart of Oak," or common British oak, with which our vessels should be built, is a close-grained, firm, solid timber, rarely subject to rot, and indigenous to this country.

Q. What is the other?

A. The sessile-cupped oak, said to be a foreign introduction, loose and sappy, not half so durable, and peculiarly subject to the ravages of dry rot.

Q. Is there not a difference of opinion on this subject?

A. Yes; some writers consider both kinds of oak of equal durability and hardness, but that they are liable to be greatly deteriorated when planted in certain soils.

Q. Is not the bark of the oak useful?

A. Yes; the tanner and dyer could not do without it; the very saw-dust also is serviceable to them.

Q. Are not even the ashes of it useful?

A. Yes; to cleanse and purify wine, and for mixing with hard water to soften it for washing.

Q. What are the roots suitable for?

A. Handles for hammers, knives, &c.

Q. Is the fruit called the acorn fit to be eaten?

A. Yes; it supplies food for deer and hogs; and when bruised, poultry will thrive upon it.

Q. Did not man, before the cultivation of corn, feed upon acorns?

A. Yes; when the Saxons ruled over England, acorns were the riches of the land; a dearth of acorns was regarded then as a calamity equal to a dearth of corn now.

Q. Did they not also depend upon them for the fattening of swine?

A. Yes; of which large herds were fed in every forest, under the conduct of a swineherd, who tended them during the day, and summoned them by the blast of a horn at nightfall.

Q. Is oak-bark valuable in medicine?

A. Very much so.

Q. Is it not also in request for forming hot-beds for the growth of pines?

A. Yes; and the branches of the oak, as well as of several other trees, are burned for charcoal.

Q. How is the age of this noble tree ascertained?

A. By counting the rings in its trunk when felled; for it forms a fresh ring every year till it arrives at perfection, and it is generally as many years in decaying.

Q. Was not a noted oak felled in 1810?

A. Yes; it was called the large Golenos oak; it grew near Newport, in Monmouthshire, and was 28½ feet in circumference.

Q. What was its age?

A. Its rings amounted to 400, a proof that this tree had not ceased growing for 400 years.

Q. What was its value when felled?

A. The bark brought 200*l.*, and its timber 670*l.*

Q. Which is the oldest oak in England?

A. One called the *Parliament Oak*, from the tradition of Edward I. holding a parliament under its branches: the tree is supposed to be fifteen hundred years old.

Q. Where does it stand?

A. In Clipstone Park, belonging to

the Duke of Portland ; it is the most ancient park in the island, having existed before the Conquest.

Q. Where is the tallest oak in England ?

A. At Welbeck Abbey, in Nottinghamshire, the property of the same nobleman ; it is called " *The Duke's Walking Stick*," and is 112 feet high.

Q. Is not Welbeck Abbey noted for extraordinary oaks ?

A. Yes ; the *Greendale Oak* is the largest : its branches cover a space of 700 square yards ; a coach-road is cut through this aged tree. The *Two Porters*, 100 feet high, stand near one of the entrances to the park, like sylvan deities ; also another called the *Seven Sisters*, from which spring seven stems 90 feet in height, and many others of astonishing dimensions.

Q. Which is the largest oak in England ?

A. The Calthorpe Oak, in Yorkshire ; it measures 78 feet in circumference where the oak meets the ground.

Q. What is wainscoting?

A. The wood of the Dutch oak; it is beautifully grained, and when polished forms an elegant wooden lining for rooms.

Q. But is not the term wainscoting applied generally to all wooden linings for rooms?

A. Yes; cedar, mahogany, and even deal being often used.

Q. What kind of tree is the elm?

A. It is second only to the oak in size and beauty.

Q. What is its wood particularly used for?

A. All purposes which are to bear the extremes of wet and dry; such as water-works, mills, pipes, pumps, and coffins.

Q. Are not frames for pictures, and other carved work, made of elm?

A. Yes; because it rarely warps.

Q. What do you mean by warp?

A. To swell, or shrivel, and bend, as other wood does when it is not dry.

Q. Have not the dried leaves of the elm been used as food for cattle?

A. Yes; when there has been a scarcity of hay or other fodder. The young leaves will feed silk-worms.

Q. Is not charcoal made of elm nearly as good as that of oak?

A. Yes.

Q. Is not the ash, next to the oak, of very general use?

A. It is: for it serves the soldier for spear-handles; the carpenter and wheelwright for ploughs, harrows, axle-trees, &c.; and the waterman for oars.

Q. How does that beautiful writer, Bernard Gilpin, notice the oak and the ash?

A. He styles the oak the *Hercules*, and the ash the *Venus*, of the forest: the ash is also called the "*husbandman's tree*," for its celebrity in agricultural and domestic implements.

Q. Did the ancients make any use of the bark of the ash and lime-tree?

A. Yes; before the invention of paper they made use of the inner and finer bark, called papȳrus, for writing upon.

Q. Was it more durable than paper?

A. It is supposed so, for there are manuscripts written on it still to be seen, though upwards of a thousand years old.

Q. What did the Romans call this skinny substance?

A. *Liber*, which is the Latin word for *a book*, and from whence *Library*, and *Librarian*, and the French word *Livre*, are derived.

Q. From what language do we derive the word *book?*

A. From the Danish word *bog*, which was the beech-tree, because that being the most plentiful in Denmark, was used to engrave on.

Q. Were their books in appearance like ours?

A. No; they were rolled upon a pin, and placed erect, titled on the outside in red letters, and appeared like a number of small pillars on the shelves.

Q. Of what particular use is the bark of trees?

A. It defends them from injury, and preserves them from cold.

Q. Why do evergreens preserve their leaves during the winter ?

A. Because their barks are of a more oily quality than those of other trees.

Q. What is the wood of the beech-tree used for ?

A. The upholsterer forms it into chairs, stools, bedsteads, &c.; dishes and trays are also made of it.

Q. Is the bark of this tree useful for any thing ?

A. Yes; for floats for fishing nets, instead of corks.

Q. Is it not very subject to the worm ?

A. It is; and this unfits it for purposes where duration is requisite; but for band-boxes, hat-cases, &c., it is very useful.

Q. Are not the leaves said to be useful ?

A. Yes; when gathered in autumn, they make the best and easiest mattresses.

Q. In what countries are they much used for this purpose ?

A. In Denmark and Switzerland;

they will keep for seven or eight years, and are much superior to straw mattresses.

Q. Do not many creatures feed upon the fruit of this tree?

A. Yes; deer, squirrels, thrushes, blackbirds, and mice; it is also said to render the flesh of pheasants very delicate.

Q. Of what use is the poplar?

A. It is a very fast-growing tree, useful for all sorts of white wooden vessels; it is very light, and makes soles as well as heels for shoes.

Q. By whom is the walnut-tree valued?

A. By the gun-maker, for the stocks of guns; also by the joiner and cabinet-maker, for its beautiful colour and grain.

Q. What use do they chiefly make of it?

A. To embellish works by inlaying them with this variegated wood.

Q. In what country is this wood in universal use?

A. In France.

Q. Is not the fruit of this tree in great request?

A. Yes; before it is ripe it is made into a pickle generally liked, and the nut when ripe is delicious.

Q. I think the sweet chestnut is the next you mentioned; what have you to tell me of that beautiful tree?

A. It is valued by the carpenter next to the oak; many of our ancient houses in London are built of it; also the roof of Westminster Hall.

Q. But has it not one great defect?

A. Yes; it frequently appears sound without when decayed within; which makes it yield to the oak in value.

Q. You have told me that ships are built of oak, but I cannot think that the body of an oak is either tall or straight enough to make the masts.

A. No; the masts are made of fir, or pine, which are tall, straight trees.

Q. What country is famous for producing them?

A. Norway, and the northern parts

of Europe. When at perfection they attain a height of 150 feet. An inferior kind is obtained from America.

Q. What is the timber of these trees called?

A. Deal; which is much used for floors and wainscots.

Q. Are these trees valuable for their timber only?

A. No; turpentine, pitch, rosin, and tar are made from them.

Q. How are these various articles obtained?

A. In the spring they make incisions through the bark of the pine-tree, and cut a hole at the bottom to receive the sap or juice, which then runs out freely.

Q. What does this form?

A. Common turpentine; it is chiefly brought from America and the Baltic.

Q. How is oil of turpentine obtained?

A. By distilling the common turpentine.

Q. Is there not a thick matter which

A a

settles at the bottom of the still in which it is prepared ?

A. Yes ; and this is yellow rosin.

Q. Is the tree good for any thing when they have drained it of all the juice or sap ?

A. Yes ; for it is then cut down, and hewn into billets, with which they fill a pit dug in the earth, and then set them on fire.

Q. What purposes does this answer?

A. Whilst burning there runs from them a black, thick matter, which is tar.

Q. What is pitch ?

A. Only tar boiled with a certain quantity of water ; sometimes an equal portion of coarse rosin is melted with it.

Q. What does pitch mixed with rosin and a small quantity of oil or tallow make ?

A. Shoemakers' wax.

Q. What does it form when mixed with whale-fat ?

A. Carriage-grease.

Q. When were coaches introduced into England ?

A. In 1580, by Fitzalan, Earl of Arundel, and at first were only drawn by a pair of horses, but the favourite Buckingham began to have them drawn by six.

Q. When were carriages generally used in England ?

A. In the reign of James I.; there were also hackney coaches, but they were so cumbrous and jolting, that they were more like waggons.

Q. How many did they hold ?

A. Eight persons, three on each seat opposite to each other, and two who sat back to back on two stools that faced the doors.

Q. When were coaches introduced into France ?

A. In the reign of Henry II. of France, about 1550; for a long time there were only three coaches in Paris, and it was considered very effeminate to be seen in one.

Q. What great hero was more timid than a woman in a coach ?

A. Henry IV. of France; for it had

been foretold by an astrologer that he should die in one.

Q. Was this prediction verified?

A. Yes; for he was stabbed by Ravaillac during a state procession, May the 14th, 1610.

Q. How did he reach him?

A. He jumped upon the hind wheel, and plunged a knife into the breast of the king, who was reading a letter.

Q. What queen used the first coach with glass instead of leather doors and curtains?

A. Catherine of Medicis. If the carriage of Henry IV. had had glass windows it might have saved his life.

Q. When were sedan-chairs brought into England?

A. In the reign of James I.; the famous Duke of Buckingham first used one.

Q. Did he not give great offence to the people by it?

A. Yes; for they thought it degrading to men to do the work of horses.

Q. Are there not some other sorts of wood you have not mentioned?

A. Yes; the lime and the willow, box and holly.

Q. What is the lime or linden tree?

A. One of the most beautiful and useful among trees, equal in age and size to the oak : its timber is remarkable for softness, lightness, toughness, and durability, so that it is most valuable to turners and carvers in wood.

Q. Where does it flourish?

A. All over Europe and Asia; its flowers afford delicious food for bees : it was much cultivated by the Hebrews in Judea, as where honey was so valuable it became of great importance.

Q. By what name is it called in the Bible?

A. The teil-tree: there are two or three species of it; one kind growing in Brazil is called *shoe-wood*, because the soles of the clogs universally worn by the Portuguese in the rainy season are made of it. At Madras they build their surf-boats of it.

Q. Is not the bark of great importance in these countries?

A. Yes; cordage, sacking, and other

things of the kind are manufactured of
it, and it is from the soft inner part that
the useful garden mat is woven.

Q. By what name are these mats
known ?

A. They were called Dutch or Bass
mats, because then imported from Holland; but they now have the proper
name of Russian mats, because they
come direct from where they are made.

Q. Are not these mats of very ancient
manufacture ?

A. Yes; and they served for bedding,
clothing, and sails for vessels; also for
the same purposes we use them for.

Q. What are willow-twigs used for ?

A. They are made into baskets, bird-
cages, cradles, and all sorts of wicker-
work.

Q. Are not osiers a sort of willow ?

A. Yes; they are a kind of low willow, found by the water-side, used for
making baskets, hampers, hurdles, &c.

Q. Must not the osier be peeled
when wanted to make fancy baskets,
mats, &c. ?

A. Yes; and the English excel in this work: for even in the time of the Romans, British baskets were among the luxuries of the Roman grandees.

Q. What sort of wood is box?

A. It is remarkable for its hardness, weight, and readiness to take a polish.

Q. What is it used for?

A. The turner finds it most valuable for mathematical instruments, pegs, screws, tops, chessmen, &c.

Q. Is not box of great importance now?

A. Yes, for engraving upon; all the fine wood prints are done on box-wood.

Q. What does the holly afford?

A. The whitest wood of any: it is hard and close-grained, and is much used in veneering, and making dressing-boxes, and other fancy works.

Q. What is bird-lime?

A. It is prepared from the bark of the holly, which is full of a slimy substance.

Q. Was the holly esteemed by the ancient Romans?

A. Yes; it was customary with them

to send branches of holly to their friends with new year's gifts, as emblematical of *good wishes*.

Q. Do we not also, in some measure, keep up the old custom?

A. Yes; for we decorate our houses and churches at Christmas with it, by way of rejoicing, and giving an air of spring in the depth of winter.

Q. What country produces mahogany?

A. It is a most noble and beautiful tree which abounds in the southern parts of East Florida, and Honduras, and in the islands of Cuba, Jamaica, and Hispaniola.

Q. Where are these islands?

A. In the West Indies, which are a set of islands in the Caribbean Sea, between North and South America.

Q. Which island produces the finest mahogany?

A. Jamaica; it admits a high polish, and is generally used for tables, chairs, &c.

Q. Is not the profit arising from mahogany very great?

A. Yes; for one tree has been known to produce upwards of 1000*l.* sterling.

Q. What do cabinet-makers call the best mahogany?

A. Spanish; from the settlements where it grows having belonged to the Spaniards; the inferior sort is called Honduras.

Q. Are there not many species of cedar-trees?

A. Yes; the ancients valued them very highly; Solomon's temple and palace were both built of this beautiful sweet-scented wood.

Q. What mountains were famous for these trees?

A. Mount Libanus in Turkey in Asia, between Syria Proper and Palestine.

Q. Is there not a chain of mountains bearing this name?

A. Yes; they are so high that they are almost always covered with snow; but the valleys are very fruitful.

Q. What did the ancients call this part?

A. Cœlo-Syria.

Q. Will this scented wood bear any polish?

A. No; but on account of its powerful smell it is much used for lining drawers and cabinets; the smell also prevents moths, insects, &c.

Q. Was not the yew-tree much cultivated by our ancestors?

A. Yes; for before the introduction of fire-arms, they manufactured their long-bows of this hard, smooth, tough wood.

Q. Was not the long-bow, which every Englishman was obliged to have, of a height equal to his own stature?

A. Yes; and it required such an extraordinary degree of strength and skill, that it was the proud boast of the yeoman, that none but an Englishman could bend that powerful weapon.

Q. What is ebony?

A. A black and valuable wood found in a particular species, only in the centre of the tree; in this kind the outside wood is white and soft, but it decays and leaves the black untouched.

Q. Where does ebony grow?

A. In the Mauritius, Ceylon, and the East Indies; it is much valued by cabinet-makers for inlaying and other ornamental work.

Q. What is the larch?

A. An elegant fir-tree, a native of the Alps, Apennines, and the mountains of Germany, Russia, and Siberia: it is also much grown in Scotland.

Q. Do they not flourish best in clumps, and in a bad soil?

A. Yes; else they become too luxuriant, and top-heavy.

Q. Is larch a very useful wood?

A. Yes; the Russians use no other for ship-building; and it is well calculated for all works exposed to the weather.

Q. But is it as durable as the oak of which our ships of war are built?

A. No; and we may consequently rely as much on the superiority of our vessels as on the bravery of our gallant sailors.

Q. Will not larch admit of a fine polish?

A. Yes ; and contributes to give uncommon lustre to any colouring laid
upon it.

Q. Do not the Italians make use of
it for picture frames ?

A. Yes ; and this is the reason why
the Italian gilding is so much better
than ours.

Q. What great painter used it for his
pictures ?

A. Raphael.

Q. Is not the wood of the laburnum
very beautiful ?

A. Yes ; it is like the dark colour of
the cocoa-nut shell, when it is polished.

Q. What is rose-wood ?

A. A beautiful wood of a dark colour,
much used by cabinet-makers for fashionable furniture in preference to mahogany.

Q. Where does it grow ?

A. In the island of Jamaica, and the
Brazils in South America.

Q. By what name is it known in the
Brazils ?

A. It is there called the Jacaranda-tree.

Q. Is there not a tree called the arbutus?

A. Yes; it was introduced into England from the Levant about 1724.

Q. Does it not grow in abundance in some parts of Ireland?

A. Yes; especially about the beautiful lakes of Killarney; it is made into very ornamental furniture.

Q. What is the teak-tree?

A. A most valuable timber-tree, called the oak of the eastern world, employed generally there for ship-building.

Q. What renders it of such great value in India for ship-building?

A. Because the English oak-tree will not grow there; it is not injured by the water, and its bitterness preserves it from worms.

Q. Of what place in Asia is it a native?

A. Of Pegu; but it flourishes luxuriantly on the coast of Malabar, and about Calcutta, and in all parts of Bengal.

Q. Is it not of very rapid growth?

A. Yes; and at all ages the wood

appears excellent, which is very different from the oak, which requires so many years to arrive at perfection.

Q. What is sandal-wood?

A. An Indian tree of Siam, and the coast of Malabar; it is burnt in small billets in India, on account of its fragrance.

Q. Is it not also used for many purposes of ornament?

A. Yes; fans, tooth-pick cases, and many toys are made of it, and a most exquisite perfume is extracted from it.

Q. Is it not sometimes used by the Chinese for coffins for their great men?

A. Yes; and they perfume both their persons and houses with it.

Q. What is satin-wood?

A. The wood of a beautiful tree growing in the Brazils, and the island of Jamaica, much valued by the upholsterers and cabinet-makers for inlaying.

Q. What is the plane-tree?

A. A noble tree much valued by the

Greeks and Romans; on account of its grateful shade they planted avenues of it to all their magnificent buildings.

Q. Is it a hardy tree?

A. Yes; it grows rapidly; and will flourish in any common soil.

Q. What is the sycamore-tree?

A. A handsome tree, which, it is remarkable, flourishes best near the sea, the spray from which does not injure it.

Q. What is the common maple?

A. A low tree, common in woods and hedges: so much valued by the Romans, that they gave an extravagant price for it for their tables.

Q. If the Romans reproached their wives for extravagance in jewels, &c., what used the latter to do?

A. To "*Turn the tables*" upon their husbands, that is, to put them in mind of what they spent upon their tables of this wood.

Q. Is it not a very light wood?

A. Yes; and on that account it is often used for violins and musical instruments.

Q. Is there not a tree called the sugar-maple?

A. Yes; a large and beautiful tree of North America; it yields a sweet juice which is made into sugar.

Q. How is the juice procured?

A. By tapping the tree; the season of doing it is February, March, and April; but it depends upon the weather, for warm days and frosty nights are most favourable for the discharge of the sap.

Q. What quantity is obtained from a tree in one day?

A. It varies greatly, even from five gallons to as little as a pint, according to the greater or less heat of the air.

Q. How long does the sap continue to flow?

A. From four to six weeks, according to the severity of the weather.

Q. Does not tapping the tree injure it?

A. On the contrary, the oftener it is tapped, the more syrup is obtained from it. A single tree has not only survived, but flourished after being tapped forty-two times in the same number of years.

Q. What is the cypress-tree?

A. A dark evergreen tree, which takes its name from the island of Cyprus, in the Mediterranean, where it still grows in great luxuriance.

Q. To what heathen god is it consecrated on account of its gloomy appearance?

A. To Pluto: it was used at the funerals of people of eminence, and branches of it were placed before the houses in which persons lay dead.

Q. Was it valued as a wood by the ancients?

A. Most highly; it takes a fine polish, is of a pale reddish colour, with deep veins, and is very durable.

Q. What famous doors were formed of it?

A. Pliny tells us the doors of the temple of Diana, at Ephesus, were made of it, and they were 400 years old when he wrote, and as good as new.

Q. Were not the gates of St. Peter's at Rome said to be of cypress?

A. Yes; and were more than a thousand years old when they were removed, to be replaced by brass ones.

Q. Is not the bread-fruit tree a very remarkable one?

A. Yes; it grows wild in Otaheite, and other islands of the South Seas, and is about the size of our largest apple-trees.

Q. What is the fruit like?

A. It grows on the boughs like apples, but it is as large as a penny loaf; it has a thick rough rind, and is gathered while green and hard.

Q. How is it prepared for eating?

A. It is baked or roasted, when the inside is found soft, tender, and white, like the crumb of new bread.

Q. Will it keep?

A. No; it must be eaten new, for if it be kept above twenty-four hours it grows harsh and choky.

Q. How long does it last in season?

A. Eight months in the year, during which the natives eat no other sort of bread.

Q. Were not great pains taken to propagate it in the West Indies?

A. Yes; but it has not hitherto answered the expectations that were entertained of it, the negroes having a greater relish for the banana, or plantain.

Q. Is there not in Bambara, in the interior of Africa, a tree called the micadia, or butter-tree?

A. Yes; it yields abundance of a kind of vegetable marrow, pleasant to the taste, and highly esteemed by the natives.

Q. What sort of a tree is it?

A. It is not unlike our oak, and it produces a nut enveloped in an agreeable pulpy substance, about the size of our chestnut.

Q. How is it prepared for use?

A. The nuts are exposed in the sun to dry, after which they are pounded very fine, and boiled in water.

Q. What is the result?

A. The oily particles contained in the nuts soon float on the surface; when cool, they are skimmed off, and then made into little cakes for use.

Q. Who gives us this account?

A. Lander, the enterprising African traveller.

Q. What European has recently explored for the first time the interior of South Africa?

A. Our enterprising countryman, Dr. Livingstone; and he has written a most interesting account of his travels.

Q. Did he not find this region very productive?

A. Yes; vegetation flourishes most wonderfully; and if the people were more civilized, they might produce cotton, and many other things useful in commerce.

Q. Is there not a curious tree mentioned by Humboldt, called the *Palo de Vaca*, or cow-tree?

A. Yes; it grows in Columbia, in America, on the barren side of a rock; its branches appear dead and dried, yet when the trunk is pierced, there flows from it a sweet and nourishing milk.

Q. When is this vegetable fountain most abundant?

A. At sunrise, when the blacks and natives hasten from all quarters with large bowls to receive it.

Q. Should we not adore God for the kind provision and comfort He furnishes, in all countries, for His creatures?

A. Yes.

Q. What tree is the pride of Hindostan?

A. The banian-tree, or Indian fig-tree, which they plant near their Hindoo temples. The size of some of these trees is stupendous. Sir James Forbes mentions one which has 350 *large* trunks, the smaller stems exceeding 3300; one tree has been known to shelter an army of 7000 men.

Q. Is its foliage beautiful?

A. Very; the leaves are large, soft, and of a lively green; the fruit a small, bright, scarlet fig.

Q. What is bamboo?

A. An Indian reed full of dark spots, which look like joints; the reeds sometimes grow to the height of a hundred feet; they are also found in some parts of America.

Q. What is their principal use ?

A. The ancients valued them for their sweet juice, which served them for sugar, and the young shoots they pickled.

Q. When the stalks were old, did they not use them in building ?

A. Yes ; as well as for making many articles of furniture : and as the reed is quite hollow, they served them also for water-pipes.

Q. What is done with the lesser stalks ?

A. They are made into a great variety of ornamental walking-canes, called rattans ; and the people of Otaheite make flutes of them.

Q. Is there not a great variety of foreign animals whose skins and furs are very valuable ?

A. Yes : their furs are used for muffs, tippets, flounces, linings for mantles, hammercloths, &c.; and their skins are prepared by the tanner into leather.

Q. Which are the most valuable furs ?

A. The ermine, sable, and chinchilla.

Q. What sort of animal is the ermine or stoat?

A. A beautiful little creature resembling the weasel, found in the northern parts of Siberia, Russia, Norway, and Lapland.

Q. How are they caught?

A. Generally in traps, baited with flesh; but they are sometimes shot with blunt arrows that their skins may not be injured.

Q. When do they hunt them?

A. In the winter, because their hair, which is as yellow as gold in summer, then turns as white as snow, except the tip of their long and bushy tail, which is as black as jet.

Q. Does not this circumstance often enable them to escape from their enemies?

A. Yes; for being of the colour of the snow of these cold countries, they are not very easily seen.

Q. Is this not a proof of the kindness of the Almighty for all His creatures?

A. Yes.

Q. Why is the fur of these little animals so highly valued?

A. Because for many centuries past it has been used for lining the robes of our kings and nobles; and the black tips of the tails are very ornamental, valuable, and beautiful.

Q. Do not the ladies have muffs, tippets, &c., of ermine?

A. Yes.

Q. Why are they so expensive?

A. Because it takes so many skins to make any thing; each little tail belongs to a whole skin.

Q. What is the sable?

A. A small animal resembling the marten and weasel; the fur is very valuable, and of a deep glossy brown, black at the ends.

Q. Where is it found?

A. In Siberia, Kamschatka, the vast forests of Russia, and in the northern parts of America.

Q. How are these animals taken?

A. Generally in traps, and snares, to

avoid hurting their skins, which are sold for large sums.

Q. Are not the dark skins the most esteemed?

A. Yes; their value greatly depends upon their colour.

Q. By whom is this animal hunted?

A. Either by criminals, whom the Russian government has banished, or by soldiers sent for that purpose.

Q. Do not these hunters go through great hardships, fatigue, and peril?

A. Yes; for they hunt them in the winter, as their skins are then in the highest perfection; and the cold they have to endure is intense.

Q. Are they sprightly, active little creatures?

A. Very much so; they form holes or burrows underground, where they repose all day, and they ramble about all night.

Q. Are sable muffs, tippets, and trimmings much esteemed?

A. Yes; and they are very expensive.

Q. Were not furs considered by

our ancestors as a necessary part of dress?

A. Yes; for the distinction of rank was expressly shown by the kind of fur displayed on their dress. Ermine and sable were reserved exclusively for the principal nobility of both sexes.

Q. You have mentioned the marten, what sort of animal is it?

A. A small quadruped of the weasel tribe, about eighteen inches long, valuable for its fur.

Q. What is its colour?

A. A blackish tawny colour; the most valuable part of the skin is that which extends along the middle of the back.

Q. What is it used for?

A. It is in great request in Europe for lining and trimming the robes of magistrates; and the Turks, who are very choice in their furs, particularly admire it.

Q. From whence are these skins imported?

A. Principally from Hudson's Bay

and Canada; like the ermine and sable, they are the finest in winter.

Q. What is the chinchilla?

A. A small creature of the rat tribe, which has a beautiful soft grey fur.

Q. Where does it come from?

A. It is a native of South America; and the Peruvians used to spin the hair of it into a fine delicate texture like wool, which they valued highly.

Q. Has not the skin of the chinchilla of late years been in much request in this country?

A. Yes; in consequence of its having become a fashionable and favourite article for ladies' muffs.

Q. Do not swans'-down muffs and tippets rank next after these valuable furs?

A. Yes; these delicate articles are formed of the skins of the wild swan, dressed with the down upon them.

Q. Where do these valuable and elegant creatures abound?

A. In the northern hemisphere, about Iceland, Kamschatka, and Lapland;

they afford the inhabitants of these cold regions their beautiful down for warm clothing.

Q. What countries furnish England with this beautiful material?

A. It is principally imported from Dantzic and the Baltic: and the Orkney and Shetland isles also share in the trade.

Q. Were not these stately birds highly esteemed by our ancestors?

A. Yes; at Archbishop Neville's feast in the reign of Edward the Fourth, four hundred of these birds were dressed.

Q. Are they eaten now?

A. No; only the cygnets, or young swans; many of these are fatted in Norfolk for Christmas feasts.

Q. What is the eider-down?

A. The fine white down which grows upon the breast of the eider-duck.

Q. How is it procured?

A. They plunder the nests of these affectionate creatures, who pluck it from their own breasts to line them.

Q. What is its use?

A. To stuff cushions or pillows, and for making beds, which are used in very cold countries instead of the common quilt.

Q. Where are these birds found?

A. In the northern parts of Europe, Asia, and America: they form their nests on small islands not far from the sea-shore.

Q. Have not squirrel-skins been much in request of late for muffs and tippets?

A. Yes; there is a great variety of squirrels, the red, grey, black, and white; the grey skins used in England for muffs come in large quantities from Russia and Siberia.

Q. What is minever fur, so often mentioned as a part of the dress in our early reigns?

A. It is said to have been the skin of the under part of the squirrel, or that of the white weasel.

Q. Is not the skin of the fitch, or polecat, used for common muffs, &c.?

A. Yes; it is a small animal, the hair coarse and of two colours, the middle being tawny and the ends black. It is said to breed the moth.

Q. Where are the skins of polecats imported from?

A. Germany and Poland.

Q. Are bear-skins very useful?

A. Yes; of all coarse furs these are the most valuable; at Petersburgh and Moscow they form one of the most costly articles in the winter wardrobe of a man of fashion.

Q. What is the colour of bear-skin?

A. Black; except in Greenland, where it is always white.

Q. To what purposes are they applied in this country?

A. A few years ago they were fashionable for muffs; but now they are in esteem only for hammercloths, housings, caps, gloves, &c.

Q. What do you mean by housings?

A. Horse-cloths, put under the saddles of military men, and other ornaments of a cavalry horse, such as pistol-holsters, &c.

Q. From whence are bear-skins usually imported ?

A. From North America, though they are found in Europe, Asia, and India.

Q. Is not the hunting of bears a principal employment of the inhabitants where they are found?

A. Yes ; and it is a most profitable pursuit.

Q. Is not the leather made from bear-skins very useful ?

A. Yes ; it is made into harness for carriages, and other purposes where strength is required.

Q. Is not every part of the bear useful ?

A. Yes ; its flesh is excellent food, something like pork ; its paws are esteemed a great delicacy, even at the emperor's table ; and the hams are salted and dried, and sent to all parts of Europe.

Q. Is not the fat valuable ?

A. Yes ; an oil is made from it, used

for making the hair grow, and it has been found beneficial in cases of rheumatism.

Q. Do not the Russians and Kamschatkans esteem it as good as olive oil with their food?

A. Yes.

Q. What are fox-skins?

A. A soft and warm brown fur, which in many parts of Europe is used for muffs and tippets, for the linings of winter garments, and for robes of state.

Q. Is not this animal found in almost every country in the world?

A. Yes; but the fur that is principally brought to this country comes from North America.

Q. Are there not black, grey, blue, red, and white foxes?

A. Yes; but the black is reckoned the most valuable, on account of its scarcity and beauty.

Q. Is not fox-hunting a favourite diversion in this country?

A. Yes.

Q. What is the badger?

A. A small animal of the bear tribe, covered with long, coarse hair like bristles.

Q. For what purpose is its skin useful?

A. When dressed with the hair on, it makes excellent knapsacks and covers for travelling trunks, &c.

Q. Are not the hairs or bristles made into brushes for painters?

A. Yes. This animal is found in the woody parts of England and Europe; and it is about the size of a small pig.

Q. What are leopard-skins esteemed for?

A. Principally as furniture for war-horses, hammercloths, &c.; the skin is very beautiful, of a deep yellow colour, studded over with black or dark spots.

Q. Of what country is the leopard a native?

A. Of Africa; it is found principally in Senegal and Guinea; but there are leopards in Persia, India, and China.

Q. Is it not extremely savage?

A. Yes; and it is caught, like the tiger and lion, by digging deep pits which are lightly covered over.

Q. Is it not a mark of the kindness of the Creator, that these savage beasts go in search of prey during the night?

A. Yes; for in the day, when man is abroad, they usually sleep in their dens.

Q. What are the skins of seals used for?

A. The coverings of trunks and making of caps; they are a large amphibious quadruped, caught in the north and south polar seas.

Q. Where are they usually found?

A. In the hollows of rocks or caverns near the sea.

Q. Are not these animals very watchful?

A. Yes; they seldom sleep longer than a minute without moving, for having no external ears, they would otherwise be liable to surprise from enemies.

Q. Is not seal-skin made into a valuable leather for shoes?

A. Yes.

Q. What does the wolf afford us?

A. Nothing valuable but its skin, which makes a warm and durable fur; it is a ferocious animal of the dog tribe.

Q. Were not wolves once very numerous in England?

A. Yes; but by the care of kings Edgar and Edward I. they were entirely destroyed.

Q. Was not the skin of the lion considered a badge of great honour?

A. Yes; it was formerly used as the tunic of heroes; it now serves both as a mantle and bed for many of the African tribes.

Q. What do you mean by a tunic?

A. A sleeveless coat or vest.

Q. Did not the Romans tame this noble beast in a wonderful manner?

A. Yes; for Mark Antony, the Roman triumvir, was publicly drawn in his chariot by lions.

Q. What people value tiger-skins very highly?

A. The Chinese; the mandarins cover their seats of justice and sedans with them, and use them for cushions and pillows in the winter.

Q. Have not the great military officers of China the figure of a tiger embroidered on their robes?

A. Yes; and there could not be found a better symbol of the evils and horrors of war.

Q. Is not the skin of the lynx thought valuable?

A. Yes; for it has a thick soft fur, and when the spots are tolerably distinct the skins are sold at high prices.

Q. What sort of an animal is it?

A. Of the cat tribe, but four times as large as the common cat.

Q. Where are they found?

A. In the woods and forests of the northern parts of Europe, Asia, and America.

Q. Are not the skins of cats a very considerable branch of commerce in some countries?

A. Yes; as furs, they are valued for

some purposes, but those of the Spanish cats are most esteemed.

Q. What people export a great many of them ?

A. The Russians; they even send them into China.

Q. Is not the hair of the wild cat very long, and of a fine white grey ?

A. Yes; it is a savage, formidable animal, found wild in the woods of Europe, Asia, and America.

Q. Were not cats considered as sacred objects by the Egyptians ?

A. Yes; and whoever accidentally killed one was liable to severe punishment.

Q. What story does Herodotus, the Greek historian, tell us about this ?

A. That whenever a cat died a natural death, the inhabitants of the house used to shave their eyebrows in token of sorrow.

Q. What was done with the animal ?

A. It was embalmed and nobly interred.

Q. What story does Southey relate

about cats in his history of the Brazils?

A. That the first couple of cats which were carried to Cuyuba sold for a pound weight of gold.

Q. Was it not commonly thought that Whittington made his immense fortune by the sale of his cat?

A. Yes; but it was not the *whiskered mouse-killing cat*, but the coasting *coal-carrying cat*, that realized his fortune.

Q. How?

A. It was said that this worthy merchant constructed a vessel, which from its swiftness and lightness he aptly named " *a cat*," which traded between Newcastle and London with coals, and laid the foundation of great wealth.

Q. What is the ichneumon?

A. A quadruped, found in Egypt and Asia, being in both places highly valued.

Q. Why?

A. Because it is the natural enemy of the whole serpent race: it will fight the most venomous of them, and seize them by the throat without receiving any injury itself.

Q. Is it not also a great enemy to the crocodile?

A. Yes; for it digs its eggs out of the sand and hills, and devours great numbers of the young ones.

Q. For these services was it not ranked by the ancient Egyptians amongst their deities?

A. Yes; and received divine honours.

Q. Was this formidable creature easily tamed?

A. Yes; and was kept in houses like a cat, and destroyed the rats and mice in the same manner.

Q. What is the ostrich?

A. An immense bird, found in Asia and Africa.

Q. What is it valuable for?

A. The Arabs hunt it for the sake of the feathers of its wings and tail, which are a great article of traffic.

Q. What are these feathers esteemed for?

A. They are used for female head-dresses, and for plumes for officers' hats, &c.

Q. What people esteemed the ostrich as an article of food ?

A. The Romans. It is recorded of Heliogabālus, the infamously celebrated gourmand emperor, (whose custom it was to eat of only one dish in a day, but that a very expensive one,) that he ordered the brains of 600 ostriches to be dressed in one dish.

Q. Are not the eggs of the ostrich esteemed even among Europeans as well tasted and very nourishing ?

A. Yes ; but they are too scarce to. be fed upon, although a single egg is said to be sufficient for eight men, as it weighs about fifteen pounds.

Q. What is the bird of paradise?

A. A most beautiful bird, found in New Guinea, and the adjacent islands of Aroo.

Q. How are they caught ?

A. They are shot with blunt-headed arrows, or taken by bird-lime, or in snares.

Q. What do they do with them as soon as they are killed?

A. They cut their legs off, take out their inside, and dry them in smoke; they then send them to Banda, and other settlements, for sale.

Q. What people value them very highly?

A. The Persians and Indians: in these countries they adorn the turbans of persons of rank, the handles of sabres, and the trappings of horses.

Q. Were there not some extraordinary ideas of this bird?

A. Yes; it was thought they had no legs, that they were constantly flying, and never touched the earth till their death, and that they fed only on dew.

Q. How did these ridiculous notions arise?

A. Probably from the beautiful nature of their plumage, and their being sold without insides or legs.

Q. Who introduced them into Europe?

A. Magellan, the Portuguese navigator, who sailed round the world in 1520. He says, they were held in such veneration by the inhabitants of the Molucca Islands, as to be called by them "God's birds."

Q. Is there not something extraordinary related of their having a leader to each flock?

A. Yes; and it is quite distinct in size and plumage from the rest, being black; it is called the "king bird of paradise," there being but one in a large flock, which it is observed he always leads. They are exceedingly rare, and very seldom obtained.

Q. What is the lamprey?

A. A small eel-shaped fish, much esteemed by epicures, particularly when potted or stewed.

Q. Which of our kings died from eating too heartily of them?

A. Henry the First.

Q. What river is celebrated for them?

A. The Severn; and it was the custom of the city of Gloucester to present to the sovereign at Christmas a lamprey-pie with a raised crust.

Q. Did not the Romans set a high value on eels?

A. Yes; they considered them one of the greatest delicacies of their tables, and they were preserved and fed with the greatest care.

Q. Where are they found?

A. In both salt and fresh water, in almost every country in Europe.

Q. Were not oysters considered by the ancient Romans a great luxury?

A. Yes; Pliny relates in his time they were considered so exquisite, as, when in perfection, to have been sold for enormous prices.

Q. Who furnished the Romans with oysters?

A. The Britons; they were fetched from the neighbourhood of Sandwich. The largest are caught off the coast of Normandy, and principally supply Paris.

Q. What is the turtle?

A. A species of tortoise found in

great numbers on the sea-shore of most countries within the torrid zone.

Q. Are they not highly valued in this country?

A. Yes; for the sake of the fine soup which is made of them: they are brought to us principally from the West Indies.

Q. How are they taken?

· A. They are easily caught whilst asleep upon the shore; for the sailors go gently and turn them on their backs, and their shell is so heavy that they cannot recover their feet.

Q. What sort of creature is the locust which we read of in the Old and New Testaments?

A. It is an insect not much unlike a large grasshopper, very common in most of the eastern countries.

Q. Are they not eaten by many of these people?

A. Yes; and the Hottentots and African tribes delight in them; they make their eggs into a kind of soup, and boil the insects in milk.

Q. Is not the peacock a beautiful creature?

A. Yes; they have always been valued, and were among the treasures of the East sent to King Solomon.

Q. Did not the Romans esteem them highly for the table?

A. Yes; and in England the young pea-fowls are now thought a great delicacy.

Q. Was it not a distinguished dish in the days of chivalry?

A. Yes; and called " *the food of lovers and the meat of lords.*" On these occasions it was served up on a golden dish, and carried to table by a lady of rank, attended by a train of high-born dames and damsels, accompanied by music.

Q. Who was appointed to carve it?

A. On the occasion of a tournament the successful knight. He was obliged to regulate his portions so that each individual, be the company ever so numerous, might taste; and if he had any oath or vow to make, rising from his seat, and extending his hand over the bird, he exclaimed, " I vow to God, to the blessed Virgin, to the dames, and to the *peacock.*"

Q. How was this bird served up in Shakspeare's time?

A. In a pie; the head richly gilt, being placed at one end of the dish, and the tail spread out in its full circumference at the other, stuffed with spices and sweet herbs.

Q. By what people are their feathers much valued?

A. By the Chinese, for decorating the caps of the mandarins : *three peacock's feathers* marking the highest honour to which a Chinese mandarin can aspire. They are also valued by them for various ornamental works.

Q. How many feathers are there in the peacock's crest?

A. Twenty-four; in ancient times their crests were among the ornaments of the kings of England.

Q. Was not the heron's crest much esteemed as an ornament when the diversion of falconry was in fashion?

A. Yes; it is a slender, smooth, glossy black plume, deemed a mark of great distinction in the days of chivalry, when it was considered royal game; and it now forms the centre of the ostrich white plume which adorns the caps of the noble Knights of the Garter.

Q. Is not the elegant tuft of this bird worn as a badge of sovereignty in Persia?

A. Yes; and is placed on the right side of the head. Nelson had a superb heron's plume presented to him by the Sultan, richly set in diamonds; the highest honour he could confer upon him, as none but nobles or great commanders in Asiatic countries are permitted to wear them.

Q. What bird furnishes the military plumes?

A. That beautiful bird, the common cock of our farm-yards: the long streamy feathers of his neck and back, and the stiffer ones of his tail, are formed by industrious females into a variety of elegant shapes, according to regimental regulations.

Q. Were not plumes a distinguishing decoration in almost all European armies ?

A. Yes; with the exception of the French, who used to substitute a fringe of white feathers round the hat. The nobles of Queen Elizabeth's time and the Stuarts were distinguished for the elegance of their plumes.

Q. Pray what is the nautilus ?

A. A very scarce and curious shell shaped like a ship; the fish that steers this little bark is wonderfully made.

Q. Pray describe it.

A. It has eight legs of different length and form : these it uses as oars and rudder, and a skinny membrane it raises to ply the wind.

Q. How does it manage its little vessel ?

A. In fine weather it sails along boldly : but if fearful of danger, it returns to its shell, and sinks to the bottom.

Q. Is it not supposed that men first took the idea of sailing from what they saw done by this little creature?

A. Yes; and the word nautilus is formed from the Greek word *naus*, a ship, or *nautes*, a sailor.

Q. Is not the pinna-marina very curious?

A. Yes; it is a muscle found on the Calabrian coast sticking to the rocks.

Q. What are its habits?

A. When in search of food, it throws out a beard of a most silky and brilliant appearance, which looks like liquid gold.

Q. What is found in this curious beard?

A. Within its meshes small fish are caught, and every separate tuft contains a little crab.

Q. What are these crabs called?

A. The watchmen of the muscle, for they give notice if an enemy approach, when the muscle directly draws in its shining beard and its guard along with it.

Q. Is it not said that Lord Nelson, when stationed on the Sicilian coast, had a muff presented to him made entirely of the tufts of this beautiful beard?

A. Yes; and the value of it was estimated at five hundred pounds.

Q. Were not figures of eagles carried before the Roman legions in battle?

A. Yes; and they have been adopted as military emblems by France, Austria, Prussia, and Russia.

Q. What was the origin of the figure of Britannia?

A. The Romans, who recorded all events on medals, cast it to signalize their conquests over our island.

Q. Has it not been preserved as testifying their high opinion of us?

A. Yes; the warlike nation of Britain is shown by the female's accoutrements; she sits upon a rock, or globe, and the waves of her island home beat upon her feet.

Q. What do her spear and shield denote?

A. The·military genius of her country, and her power to defend her freedom and her rights.

Q. Was the lion assigned her by the Romans?

A. No; it was added afterwards, probably to denote the magnanimous character of her hardy sons.

INDEX.

THE END.

GILBERT AND RIVINGTON, PRINTERS, ST. JOHN'S SQUARE, LONDON

www.ingramcontent.com/pod-product-compliance
Lightning Source LLC
Chambersburg PA
CBHW031821270326
41932CB00008B/495